# THERESA CECILIA GAYNORD

# WHERE THE ROAD MEETS THE SKY

First Printing ©2025 Transcendent Zero Press

Interior Photography pages 7-11 © Loyd Williamson

Interior Photography pages 45,52,56,58,60,77,78 © Nathan Pratyksh Khanna

Interior Photography pages 66-68 © Theresa C. Gaynord


ISBN 978-1-946460-71-4

# WHAT THEY ARE SAYING

"WHERE THE ROAD MEETS THE SKY," THERESA C. GAYNORD INVITES
HER READERS ON A WHITMANESQUE JOURNEY BEYOND THE HORI-
ZON'S RIM; OSTENSIBLY PRESENTED PRIMARILY THROUGH ARCHE-
TYPAL CHRISTIAN IMAGERY, SYMBOLISM, AND TROPES, BUT THERE
ARE NODS TO WICCA, HINDUISM, VOODOO, AS WELL AS TO BOTH
GREEK AND NATIVE AMERICAN MYTHOLOGY.  AND ALL ARE GROUNDED
DEEP WITHIN THE WORLD OF NATURE, AND HUMANKIND'S SEARCH
FOR SPIRITUALITY IN THIS LIFE.  ESCHEWING THE DOGMATIC, SHE
FINDS MYSTICAL ELEMENTS IN THE WORLD AROUND HER; AND THE
OVERALL EFFECT IS BOTH UPLIFTING AND DEEPLY PROFOUND.  HER
LINES RESOUND WITH NATURAL ECHOES OF NATURAL BEAUTY THAT
ARE A JOY TO READ SILENTLY OR SPEAK ALOUD:

"INDESCRIBABLE SOFT MURMURS
SEARCH FOR A HORRIFIED LISTENER,
LISTING THEIR PRIVATE GRIEVANCES,
AS THEY GLARE.
OBJECTS OF BEAUTY, OF KIN
SURROUND AND BLANKET THE FOREST.
THERE ARE GUARDIAN SPIRITS,
FIELDS AND GROVES OF THEM,
AND ENERGIES NOT YET IDENTIFIED."
NOR DOES SHE SHY AWAY FROM THE DARKER ASPECTS OF THE HU-
MAN EXPERIENCE:
"I COULD SEE THE JAGGED MOON,
AND IT LOOKED AS IF IT HAD DIED
IN SLEEP.
IT SPOKE TO ME AND SAID,
'SWING.'
DEAD MEN RISE,
AND I'M AT THE HELM,
LEARNING THE ROPES."

"HER WORDS CAPTURE THE OVERWHELMING SENSE OF WONDER ONE

FEELS WHEN CONTEMPLATING "DISTANT FIREFLIES," "THE PHANTOM AMONG THE TREES," A CHORAL COMPOSITION BY RACHMANINOFF, OR "(T)WILIGHT FANTASIES (THAT) GLEAM/IN THE POMP OF NIGHT." THIS IS POETRY IN ITS HIGHEST FORM."

MICHAEL PENDRAGON—EDITOR AND PUBLISHER OF THE RENOWNED LITERARY HORROR JOURNAL, PENNY DREADFUL.

"THERESA GAYNORD'S SPIRITUAL ARRANGEMENTS WILL CHANGE THE WAY YOU INTERPRET YOUR SURROUNDINGS. I RETURN TO HER PROSE WHENEVER I NEED A MELODIC HAND TO HOLD AS I STRIVE TO UNDERSTAND THINGS LARGER THAN MYSELF."

SEAN DAVID HARVEY AUTHOR/GHOSTWRITER.

"WITH THE WORLD'S RELIGIONS AS ITS INSPIRATION, GAYNORD'S POEMS ARE FILLED WITH PROSE THAT STIRS AND SEARCHES THE SOULS OF ITS READERS, ELICITING EMOTIONS RARELY FELT IN POETRY TODAY. EACH ONE IS A BEAUTIFUL AND POWERFUL CHORD THAT RESOUNDS IN EACH OF US."

BEN EADS, AUTHOR HOLLOW HEART AND CRACKED SKY.

"WHERE THE ROAD MEETS THE SKY EVOKES EMOTIONS AND IMAGERY SOMETIMES SUPPRESSED. AN INCREDIBLE JOURNEY THROUGH THE IMAGINATION AND SOME OF THERESA'S BEST WORK."

STEVEN L. SHREWSBURY AUTHOR RECKONING DAY, BLADESPELL AND RED WAVES OF SLAUGHTER

IN SEARCH OF A HIGHER POWER—


A PERSONAL, SPIRITUAL JOURNEY EXPLORING THE
DIVERSITY OF RELIGIOUS BELIEFS AND ONE'S PLACE IN THE
UNIVERSE.


FROM BIRTH, THERE IS A SPIRITUAL BATTLE FOR YOUR SOUL.

SPIRITUAL WARFARE IS REAL AND YOU WILL HAVE TO FIGHT
EVERY DAY BETWEEN POSITIVE AND NEGATIVE INFLUENCES
THAT WILL ULTIMATELY AFFECT YOUR DESTINY.


SOMETIMES THE ROAD TO SALVATION BEGINS WHEN THOSE
WHO ARE NOT SEEKING HIM, FIND HIM.


### Poem by Dustin Pickering, publisher

My foolishness turned me to stone
but love broke through the hardness—
the silence is wretched but true,
and I am without holy fire.

The burning craves emptiness. Flames of origin
boast of themselves.
A cloud shivers like a star
in heated skies.


"THE LORD LOOKS DOWN FROM HEAVEN ON ALL MANKIND TO SEE IF
THERE ARE ANY WHO UNDERSTAND, ANY WHO SEEK GOD." — PSALM
14:2

# CONTENTS

LORD OF DEATH

ENTER THE KILL

THE GALLOWS

PURPLE POMP

THE SLIDING BOARD

CRYSTAL OF A DREAM

HOOKED AND ROPED

STRANGLED INTO A SCREAM

BITTER CRY

WILD REGRETS

CHAPEL OF THE DAY

ONE MUST DIE

WRITTEN IN HIS EYES

TO LOOK UPON A WINE-RED ROSE

UNHOLY GROUND

BRITTLE BONE BY NIGHT

WONDERING SKY

A BLOOM IN PRISON AIR

CANVAS ON CLOTHES

THE STARTLED SOUL

THE VILEST DEEDS

LAWS BE RIGHT

OUTCASTS ALWAYS MOURN

MEN BUILT OF SHAME

THEY SCOURGE THE STRONG

OLD AND GREY

THE FETID BREATH OF DEATH

BRACKISH WATER

THE LOVELIEST OF TREES

ALONG THE BOUGH

WOODLAND RIDE

CHERRY HUNG WITH SNOW

LIGHTFOOT LAND

COUNTRY MAIDEN

HAPPY HIGHWAYS

WHAT FATED HER TO CHOOSE HIM

THE POWER OF SOUND

TRADITION

GOD FINDS YOU

TERESITA

"IF YOU ARE THE SON OF GOD, TELL THESE STONES TO BECOME BREAD."

9

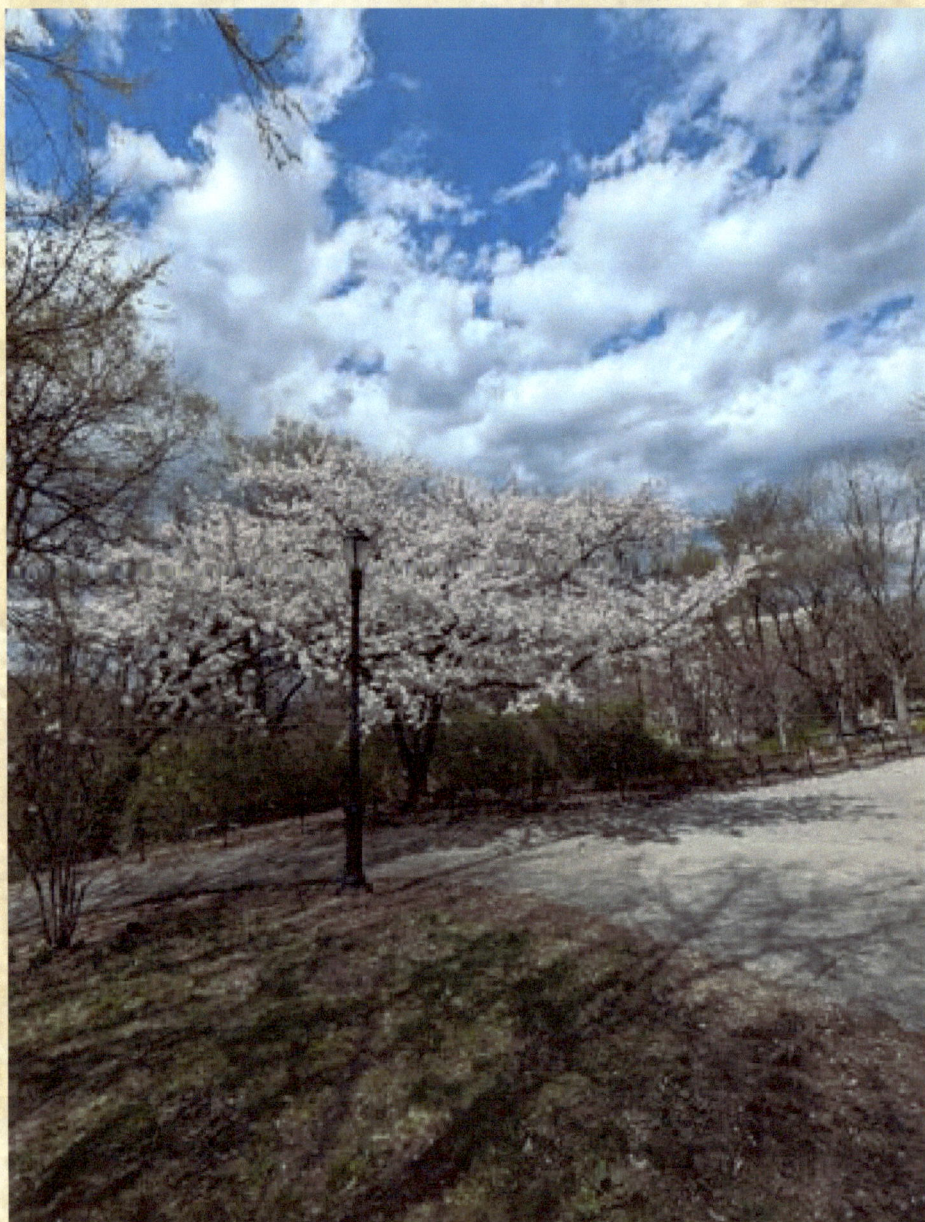

# BLOOD NOT SPILT

THE FAITHFUL SAY THERE ARE SEVEN WAYS TO SEARCH FOR GOD.
PRAYER.
NATURE SUSPENDS BIRTH BY SHAPING ITS SPIRIT, STILL AND PA-
TIENT,
IT INHABITS THE SOUL,
COILS AROUND ITS MIND,
UNTIL A SCREAM RAGES UNNOTICED.
THE WIND SWAYS GARDENS OF PEEPING FLOWERS,
A PRAYER, PROBABLY THE FIRST,
THAT PAUSES IN DEEP SILENCE.

TEMPERED WITH DELIGHT IT FRAMES IN LOW MOANS AND PLEAS,
FORMING A HOME, AN INTIMATE COTTAGE WHERE ALL CAN REST.
IT IS A SONG THAT MAKES ITS WAY OUT OF THE DARKNESS,
EVEN WHEN IT RIDES UPON A STORM SO WILD,
IT CANNOT BE TAMED.
I'VE SEEN THE BLAZING SUN IN MATTED WOODS,
WHERE THE BIRDS ARE DROWSY AND FEAR TO WAKE,
AND THE CLUSTERS OF THEIR SONGS CLING TO SILENCE.

I'VE SEEN BLOOD NOT YET SPILT WAIT IN EXILE,
BY PRAYERS WISHED IN VAIN BEYOND THE VEIL OF LONG FARE-
WELLS,
AND TEARS WEPT RETURNED TO SORROW.
CONSCIOUS VIRTUES ARE BRAVE, AND COURAGE A FOUND COMPANION
IN HOURS OF NEED.
I'VE ALSO HEARD THE SWEETNESS OF BENEDICTIONS SO NEAR,
LIKE FLOATING LILIES IN A POND,
WAYWARD YET FOUND.

IF A LITTLE FLOWER COULD ONLY UNDERSTAND ALL IN HAND,
IT WOULD ROOT ITSELF IN DEPTH AND PASSION.
IT WOULD TURN ITS EARNEST GLANCE, ONTO ITSELF,
AND NOT AWAY TOWARDS THE SUN.
AT FIRST SIGHT HOPE HALF-FLOURISHES,
AND NEVER DIES.
IT RIDES AND ROUNDS THE TERRACES OF THORNS,
CALLING OUT AS IF IT KNEW WHAT GOD AND MAN ARE.

# WHERE SOLEMN MEN WEEP

THERE ARE WORDS THAT BREAK YOUR HEART,
HEAVY UPON YOUR BROW,
A LANGUAGE YOU FALL SHORT FROM,
AN EXPECTATION THAT'S HARD TO COME BY.
SCRIPTURE
ELAPSED IN TIME FROM ANCIENT LANDS,
A JOURNEY DRESSED IN LOVE,
AND LIVES SPENT AND ARROWS PERCHED UPON

SWELLING TURF, MARKING THE SPOT
OF DEAD COMMIT,
THAT'S WHERE IT SITS,
IN BETWEEN SALVATION AND SURRENDER.
I'VE FELT THEIR VIBRATIONS,
THE WORDS OF FORGIVENESS,
THE WORDS OF JUSTICE AND TRUTH.
I'VE SLEPT BENEATH THEM, UNITED THROUGH SEPARATION.

I'VE PASSED THE GATE WITHIN A DREAM,
DESOLATE AND SICK FROM HUNGER,
OUT OF ME, WITHIN ME,
UNWORTHY AND UNKNOWN.
THERE I STOOD LISTENING TO THE ANGEL'S
HORN,
ENDURING THE SCARS OF OUTRIGHT DEFIANCE,
MY OWN SIN.

I, THE PHANTOM AMONG THE TREES,
THE GHOST BINDING WITH THE FORLORN,
WHERE SOLEMN MEN WEEP,
SLOWLY AT HIS FEET,
TREMBLING WITH THE KNOWLEDGE,
THAT ALL THINGS BREAK,
AND NOTHING IS ON FIRM EARTH.
AN AULD LANG SYNE, AMONG A SECURED LONELINESS.

## DEATH, DREAD AND DOOM

CARVED MARBLE ANGELS WITH CHEERFUL EYES,
STARE AT ME FROM EVERY CORNER.
THEY SEEM TO FOLLOW WITH WHITE BLOWN HAIR,
AND FEATHERY WINGS, AND HEARTS UPON THEIR
CHESTS.
WORSHIP
AMONG YOUNG VIRGINS,
AND VISIONS OF DELIGHT.

THEIR MUSIC WARMS ICY LIPS,
FLUSHES THROUGH WEAKENED LIMBS,
LIKE RACHMANINOFF'S COME, LET US WORSHIP.
TWILIGHT FANTASIES GLEAM,
IN THE POMP OF NIGHT.
A CIRCUMSTANCE PERCHED UPON
A CLOSING DAY,
ECHOING THROUGH MOONLIT MOUNTAINS.

I HAVE ENJOYED THEM AS MOST
ORDINARY HUMANS WOULD,
FROM AFAR.
SOMETIMES AWAY FROM HARDSHIPS TO ENDURE,
SOMETIMES OLD AND POOR AWAY FROM YOUTH,
LIKE A REMOTE CHARMER,
IN BODY, WITHOUT A LIVING SOUL,
BURDENED BY THE MYSTERY OF IT ALL.

THE APPETITE THOUGH, IT
STILL HAUNTS ME.
AND THERE'S A SAD PERPLEXITY
TO THE WAY I FEEL AND DEAL.
AND I DARE TO HOPE.
THEY FOLLOW ME FOR THE SAME REASONS,
FOR THE SAME APPETITE,
TO KNOW ME. AWAY FROM DEATH, DREAD AND DOOM.

## WEED—CLOGGED


WEEDS CAN CLOG WATERWAYS,
DISRUPT ECOSYSTEMS,
WITHOUT REPENTANCE.
I'VE EXAMINED THEM WITH HURRIED
WORD.
MORE LIKE A STAGGERING FOOL
WHO WATCHES, YET GOES ABOUT
THE DAY NEVERTHELESS.

IT'S THE LATE AFTERNOONS,
WHEN THE LIGHT IS WANING
THAT I THINK ABOUT IT ALL,
AMONG THE DISTANT PLOTTING
OF FIREFLIES THAT SWARM,
DANCING UP AND DOWN,
ILLUMINATING FACES IN SOFT AIR.
THEY COME WITH SUSTENANCE,

AND PREMONITION,
WHISPERING AMONGST THEMSELVES,
BEFORE THEY VANISH.
IT SEEMS TO ME THEY BAT THEIR LITTLE
WINGS,
JUST TO CALL US HOME.
A RETURN BETWEEN A BOLT OF LIGHTNING,
AND A BLACK OUT.

I'VE PUT ON PRETTY SHOES,
MY BEST DRESS,
AND WHITE COTTON GLOVES,
JUST TO GREET THEM.
I'VE WEDGED MYSELF FREE
FROM THE QUICKSAND TO SAVE MY OWN LIFE.
I'M THE OVERGROWN BLACKBERRY VINE
AND A DEADLY NIGHTSHADE FULL OF BERRIES.

OPEN GRAVE

I CAN SPEAK AND RECITE SCRIPTURE,
FROM GLITTER LIPSTICKED LIPS,
AND FEEL EVERY SENSE,
THE WHOLE ASPECT OF HIS BEING THAT CALLS
ME LIKE UNSUSPECTED PREY.
THE COLD DEW HELPS ME BREATHE, EVEN AS
IT TAKES AWAY MY BREATH,
SLEEPING WITH ONE EYE OPEN,


A HALF AND HALF DOZE,
IN AN OPEN GRAVE,
WHERE I FEEL AT EASE.
THERE ARE DANGEROUS INDULGENCES
I NO LONGER PERCEIVE,
EVEN THOUGH AN ELECTRIC FLASH
FORETELLS OF A PROBLEM I CAN NOT SEE.
THERE'S A CALMING PRESENCE WITH ME,

A STIRRING THAT'S VERY FAMILIAR.
HEAVEN PROMPTS ME TO USE ONE NAME.
AND IMPULSE RULES IT,
SUMMONS IT  FORTH FROM MY MOUTH.
IT IS MUTTERED LOW BETWEEN MY TEETH,
AS MY BODY ROTS,
AND MY SPIRIT LIVES.
THE DEVIL WATCHES, WITH DEADLY HATE.

I HAVE HIS MANUSCRIPT WELL
PRESERVED. EVEN AS I AM ALTERED BY
WHIMSIES,
I'VE READ AND RECITED IT.
THE DEVIL IS AWARE, AND DOESN'T LIKE IT.
HE CANNOT TRIUMPH
AGAINST THE BRIGHTNESS OF MY EYES,
IN AN OPEN GRAVE.

## SWING

MY LIPS ATE THE BODY,
DRANK THE BLOOD, IN PRAISE.
I WAS BLESSED BY THE ROARING
WINDS THAT SHOOK SAILS
AND BURST INTO LIFE
INANIMATE OBJECTS
THAT DANCED IN WAN WATERS TO
AND FRO.

THE LAZARUS HAD SAILED
TO OPEN OCEANS, A BLESSED
HOST,
FLOATING FREE AS RAIN POURED,
FROM ONE, SINGLE, SOLITARY,
BLACK CLOUD.

I COULD SEE THE JAGGED MOON,
AND IT LOOKED AS IF IT HAD DIED
IN SLEEP.
IT SPOKE TO ME AND SAID,
"SWING."
DEAD MEN RISE,
AND I'M AT THE HELM,
LEARNING THE ROPES.

THE WOODS ARE FAR AWAY,
BUT I KNOW THEY HIDE
BROOKS THAT BABBLE.
A WANDERING SPIRIT
CAN VEER OFF ITS PATH,
JUST TO LISTEN TO THEM.
BROOKS OF MISTS AND SHADOWS,
A SECOND VOICE OF PRAISE.

## THE HANGMAN


THE EARTH OOZES HOLY OIL,
A SACRED KIND OF THANKSGIVING,
WE ALL IGNORE. NATURE WARMS,
SOOTHES AS IT HEALS.
WE WEAR ITS SMUDGE.
OUR FOREHEADS ARE SMEARED
WITH ITS ESSENCE.
THE GRANDEUR OF GOD HAS SEARED

US WITH HIS TRADE.
WE STRAIN LIKE RACING LAMBS,
DAPPLED WITH DEW.
OUR TRYST, MONITORED,
FORGIVEN BY THE WOUNDS
OF CHRIST.
OUR JUSTICE CLEANSED BY THE PAIN
HE FELT,

IN THE HORROR OF ALL THINGS,
MORTAL.
THE HANGMAN, FULL OF SURRENDER,
IN BURNING TIMES,
THE SHEET OF ETERNAL FLAME,
WITH SPOTTED SHROUD,
OFFERING,
A NEW PERSPECTIVE THROUGH SACRIFICE.

# THE WOODS ARE SHUFFLING


TWIGS BREAK LIKE GLASS, AND LEAVES RUSTLE
AS IF TO WARN US THE WOODS ARE SHUFFLING.
EYES SNEAK AND HIDE, AS SERPENTS GLIDE,
HISSING GENTLY.
YET HERE, I FIND INTROSPECTION.
MAYBE NO ONE CARES THAT THE WOODS
SCREAM WITHOUT RHYME OR REASON
TO BE GIVEN.

I DON'T LIKE SUCH TALK, PERSONALLY.
FAMILIARITY BREEDS CONTEMPT,
AND I'M ONE OF THOSE RESTED OLDER
FOLKS THAT BACKS AWAY FROM UNFRIENDLY
BANTER.
I'LL BREAK THE MIRROR IF I HAVE TO,
OR IF I'M DEFINED BY IT.
THERE'S A VIRTUAL EYE THAT DOESN'T CARE

FOR IT EITHER. INDESCRIBABLE SOFT MURMURS
SEARCH FOR A HORRIFIED LISTENER,
LISTING THEIR PRIVATE GRIEVANCES,
AS THEY GLARE.
OBJECTS OF BEAUTY, OF KIN
SURROUND AND BLANKET THE FOREST.
THERE ARE GUARDIAN SPIRITS,
FIELDS AND GROVES OF THEM,

AND ENERGIES NOT YET IDENTIFIED.
THEY CALL MY NAME.TERESITA,
WALK IN OUR PATH.CHOOSE US.
YOU HAVE A WICCAN SOUL.
PERFECTION AWAITS YOU AS QUEEN.
AND THE TREES, THICK WITH FOLIAGE,
LEAVES AND BRANCHES, GREET ME.

# THE NIGHT WITH EMPTY CORRIDORS

THERE ARE CIRCLES WITH SHADED EDGES,
UPON MY WALLS AT NIGHT. THE CORRIDORS
ARE EMPTY,
AND THEY STILL SEEM TO DRIFT UPON THE PLASTER,
SOME SHRUNKEN IN SIZE, BUT GROWING.
THEY GET LARGER AND LARGER,
THEN SHRINK BACK DOWN,
REORGANIZING WITH MOVEMENT.

THEY LIKE TO CONVERGE AT MY DOOR,
LIQUID IN THEIR SIFTINGS.
I'VE SEEN THEM BEFORE,
IN BIRTH,
AND IN BRANCHES OF WISTERIA,
BLUE IN COLOR.
THEY SPEAK TO ONE ANOTHER
ABOUT ME.

SUCH LIGHTNESS IN THEIR WORDS,
AS IF THEY REMEMBERED ME,
FROM TIMES UNKNOWN.
FROM THE SOURCE OF ALL BEGINNINGS.
WHEN THEY COME, THEY SMELL
SWEET.
A CONDITION OF COMPLETE SIMPLICITY.
THEY TAKE TO MY ARMS,

BECKONING ME TO CRADLE THEM.
THEY CALL MY NAME, TERESITA,
AND SAY,
"WE ARE SO PROUD OF YOU."
"YOU ARE SO SPECIAL."
NEVER ASKING FOR ANYTHING,
YET BONDED,
TO THE INWARD TIDES OF MY SOUL.

# IRON STARS

IRON STARS CLUSTER LIKE A SET OF
SHARP KNIVES, WAITING TO
CUT THEIR VICTIMS.
YOU CAN SEE THEM THROUGH
THE OPENINGS OF ANCIENT CAVES
THAT PROTECT FROM HAIL AND RAIN,
AND HOUSE IN SACRED TRUST,
THAT WHICH WILL NOT BETRAY YOU.

IRON STARS SHINE DIFFERENTLY,
IN A DEGRADED STATE,
A MOST UNHOLY ASPECT,
THRIFTY IN ITS LIES.
SOULLESS IN ITS RUIN.
THERE ARE ADMINISTERED RITES
IN THEIR HONOR,
BASED ON A MYSTERIOUS RELIGION,

MOST WILL NOT NAME.
LABYRINTHS OF EXTRATERRESTRIALS,
OBSERVE FROM ABOVE WITH EXTREME
AVERSION.
THEY ONCE RULED HAND IN HAND WITH
THE GREAT SPIRIT,
AND BLESSED THE ABODES OF NATIVE
AMERICANS.

MY DUTIES OF MISSIONARY
HAVE HAD ME ENCOUNTER
THEIR PRESENCE.
IN THE SANGRE DE CRISTO MOUNTAINS
THEY SPOKE TO ME ABOUT THE DAWN OF REASON,
APPEALING TO MY ROMANTIC SOUL.
I FELL IN LOVE WITH THEM, TOOK EXCURSIONS
DURING THEIR ABSENCE, YEARNING FOR THEIR RETURN.

## CROWN OF FEAR

GARMENTS ARE SOILED AND HOPE IS FOILED,
AND WORDS BLOT HIS NAME,
UPON POISONED CLOTH.
A CROWN OF FEAR, TURNS INTO A CROWN
OF LOVE, IN DEATH—SOWN STREETS,
BENEATH A BLOOD RED SKY.
A PROPHECY FULFILLED,
UPON A HOLY FACE,

WHERE THE BLOOD OF STRANGLED SOULS
IS NOT RED BUT CRIMSON.
PURPLE AND BLUISH TINTS
STAIN SKIN, FILL EYES WITH ITS PASSION.
BLOOD OF ROYALTY, BLOOD OF POWER.
I, THY CHILD  KNOW WHO THOU ART.
I'VE KNELT AT YOUR FEET,
AND SPOKE TO YOU FROM MY HEART.

KING OF KINGS, I'VE SOUGHT YOU OUT.
I'VE PUT WORDS TOGETHER
ASKING FOR YOU TO FIND ME,
NEVER REALIZING YOU WERE ALWAYS
THERE,
EVEN WHEN I WAS DOING WRONG.
THERE'S A SWORD BY MY SIDE,
AND AN ARCHANGEL WHO CONQUERED MINIONS.

THERE ARE PIECES OF A PAPER UNFOLDING,
A SCROLL ALREADY WRITTEN,
IN THE HAZE OF A GOLDEN SUN.
IT STANDS FOR SOMETHING.
SOMETHING PURE.
A HOST OF BEES FLY OUT TO HAVE THEIR HONEY.
BUZZING MORE AND MORE DISTANT,
YET SO CLOSE.

# THE MEADOW-LAND

IN THE MEADOW-LAND A LARGE MAGNOLIA
TREE SITS SHINING IN THE HEAT.
THERE'S AN OLD WOODEN HOUSE
WITH COWRIE SHELLS ON THE PORCH,
AND AN INDOOR CEILING PAINTED BLUE,
A LOW COUNTRY RECIPE THAT KEEPS
EVIL SPIRITS OUT.
VOODOO DRUMS MAKE BLINDS

GO UP, AS NEIGHBORS COME OUT THE DOOR.
THERE'S A BOTTLE OF MILK,
SITTING BY A BABY'S BED,
COVERED WITH FLIES.
STAIRS CREAK, INFORMING EVERYONE
OF YOUR ENTRANCE AND YOUR EXIT.
THE FLOOR SLANTS,
IN AN ATTEMPT TO DERAIL ONE

FROM THEIR CALLING.
THESE ARE LUCKY TIMES, SOME SAY.
AND THEY SMELL OF BLUEBERRY PIE,
AND ROTTEN WOOD,
AND THEIR WORDS CLANG
WITH A DRAWL,
WITH LITTLE MONEY TO RELISH FROM.
THEY CALL TO ME WITH DANCING FEET,

AND BELLIES DISTENDED FROM
HUNGER.
A CHILD KNOCKS ON SACRED WOOD,
OPENING THE PATHS FOR THE LOAS
TO ENTER.
I LEAVE AND COME BACK
NIGHT AFTER NIGHT,
BARREN AND TREMBLING.

# THE TEARS WE SHED

THE MAKING OF AN ARTIST OR A POET,
IS BASED ON THE TEARS WE SHED
WHEN WE EXPERIENCE THEM.
IT'S IN THE WAY THEY MOVE,
THE WAY THEY TIP THEIR HAT
ALONGSIDE A GLANCE THAT DEEPENS
WITH A SMILE.
IT'S WHEN THE REVELATION

OF INNOCENT BEAUTY,
ENCOUNTERS A PURE SOUL,
ON A ROAD THAT WAS ONCE
DESOLATE,
AND UNKIND.
THE PAINTING RETREATS,
AS IF RESPONDING TO SALUTATIONS,
WHILE THE POET OPENS THE DOOR.

FATIGUE IS AN IMMEDIATE
RESPONSE,
TO THE PRESSURE OF PERFECTION,
AND THE AMUSEMENTS OF PEOPLE
NOT YET PROGRESSED.
WHAT AN EXHIBITION OF FREAKS,
WE ARE.
CALCULATED TO PROVIDE TEARS,

RATHER THAN JOY.
WE ARE SPECTACLES OF DEFORMITY,
INVENTIONS OF THE GODS
FOR AMUSEMENT.
NOTHING SPECIAL IN OUR GIFTS,
NOR OUR ARROGANCE.
WE HAVE CRUSHED GRASS ON SLOPES,
WITHOUT A SECOND THOUGHT.

# KNELT IN PRAYER

THERE ARE NO ROOTS IN REALMS OF GOLD,
WHERE WILD MANNA GROWS,
AND HONEY DRIPS IN ABUNDANCE,
AND BRAHMAN TAKES US TO KINGDOMS
YET UNSEEN.
HERE PLANETS SWIM IN THE EXPANSE
OF SPACE,
AND THE WATCHER OF THE SKIES,

IN A WILD SURMISE,
DEEMS US ALL CRAZY,
EVEN WHEN WE ARE KNELT IN
PRAYER,
AND SLUMBER IS CLOSE,
AND WOES ARE THOUGHT,
WITHIN A FINAL DREAM,
AND WE'RE FOUND,

LOITERING BY THE BANKS OF A RIVER,
FAR AWAY FROM OURSELVES,
BURNING IN A BARGE,
DISPOSED OF FOR ALL TO SEE,
DISSOLVED IN A QUIET
FORGET,
AMONG INCENSE,
AMONG INDIGENOUS

LEAVES.

KNELT IN PRAYER,
A QUEEN MOON
REMAINS ON HER THRONE
CLUSTERED AROUND BY THE FAITHFUL,
WHERE BREEZES BLOWN
EMBALM THE DARKNESS.

## PADLOCKED DOOR

BACCHUS PARTIES BEHIND A PADLOCKED
DOOR,
WHERE SAILORS DELIGHT,
OLD AND QUAINT,
LIKE SEA SAINTS,
IN CALM WATERS.
AND THE BRINE MUTTERS UNDER
ITS BREATH,

OF ANCIENT TOMBS,
AND THE MARTYRDOM OF
WINGED DRAGONS,
AND THE ABUNDANCE OF
THE HEAVENS.
SOME WORSHIP THIS,
PICTURESQUE,
AND FREE.

IF OCEANS CLEANSE,
THEY CAN HEAL,
THEY CAN OVERFLOW,
AND BECKON ANGELS
NEAR.
THEY CAN SWELL,
AND EASE US SAFELY,
INTO IMMORTALITY,

WHERE SUNSETS,
AND EVENING STARS
AWAIT,
UPON WAVES THAT SURGE,
BEFORE CRASHING
TO SHORE.
SOUND AND FOAM CRADLE,
REINCARNATE, OUT OF THE BOUNDLESS DEEP.

## THAT TROUBLED THING

THERE'S THAT TROUBLED THING CALLED
DOUBT.
IT ROAMS WITH A HUNGRY
HEART.
IT INFILTRATES
THE SOUL OF MEN.
IT BATTLES WITH
MY PEERS,

WITH MY
VALUES,
AND EXPERIENCES.
IT PENETRATES MY MIND,
TELLS ME EVERYTHING IS ADMISSIBLE,
BLURS THE BARRIERS BETWEEN
RIGHT
AND WRONG.

IT IS THE BRINGER OF ETERNAL
SILENCE,
THE SINKING STAR THAT WANTS TO DRAG YOU
ALONG.
LEAVE THE SCEPTER AND THE ISLE
BEHIND.
LISTEN TO THE TWILIGHT AND EVENING
BELL.

AND AFTER THE DARK,
REST
IN
PEACE,
IN SANE,
AND
SACRED,
DEATH.

## GREY FIGURES

THERE ARE GREY FIGURES
THAT SINK WITH THE SUN,
AND EXPAND IN STAGNANT
AIR,
FORCING A WIND-DAPPLE
HERE AND THERE,
CREATING PATCHES OF LIGHT
AND SHADOW.

IF ONLY I COULD FLY,
I WOULD JOIN THEM,
PASSING THROUGH LONE
WHEATFIELDS,
OVER ROOKS AND
BROOKS ALIKE.
I WOULD BE THE WANDERER,
SEARCHING FOR GOD,

FOR A QUIET PLACE
TO RETREAT TO.
COOL STREAMS WOULD GREET ME,
AND A HEAP OF FLOWERS
IN A MIDNIGHT STREAM
WOULD COMFORT ME.
AND SHEPHERDS WOULD
JOIN ME, FOR A WHILE.

I WOULD TEACH MYSELF,
ABOUT BEING HUSHED AND SLOW,
ABOUT LYING ALONE,
LISTENING TO MY OWN
VOICE.
I WOULD PAUSE,
BEFORE FLIGHT
AND SMILE AT THE THOUGHT.

## SAVIOR OF REMORSE

I WONDER IF GOD IS REMORSEFUL,
FOR HAVING CREATED US,
FOR SUFFERING AND DYING,
AS THE BLIND ARE DRIVEN
IN THE WRONG DIRECTION.
I OFTEN SEE HIM AS
THE SAVIOR OF REMORSE,
CRYING,

REAL TEARS,
AS WE DO HARM.
WE WEAR SUCH ENGAGING
MASKS,
BETWEEN BLURRED
SANCTITY,
AND PRIDE.
IT ALL BECOMES A PLACE

FOR US TO HIDE.
WE CLING TO GLOOM,
AND COLLECT
CIDER—APPLE HEAPS,
AND STOP THE SOUND
OF  FEET,
ACQUAINTED WITH OUR
DOWNFALL.

IS THE SAVIOR OF REMORSE
BY A COLD SPRING?
DOES HE RISE AMONG TATTERS
OF HERBS AND THORNS?
WILL HE DRINK FROM GOBLETS
LIKE THE HOLY GRAIL?
I BELIEVE IN THE ANSWERS.

# EYES OF AWE

I OBSERVED A FISSURE
IN THE EARTH'S WALL.
THERE, BY THE EDGE
OF A SMALL STONE,
IT SLITHERED.
ITS SOFT BELLY EXPELLING
SOIL.
IT'S TONGUE RIPPLING

IN AND OUT.
WITH EYES OF AWE
IT LOOKED AT ME.
WITH TWO-FORKED TONGUE
IT FLICKERED IT
IN MY DIRECTION.
I WAS ITS GUEST
AMONG THE HEAT

OF THE EARTH,
SCORCHED BY THE SUN.
AS IT WITHDREW INTO
A BLACK HOLE,
IT LOOKED BACK AT ME,
ONCE.
AS IF PROTESTING
I DID NOT FOLLOW.

I MISSED MY CHANCE,
I GUESS.
BUT TO SEE A KING IN EXILE,
UNCROWNED,
IN THE
UNDERWORLD,
WAS A HORROR
AS WELL AS A BLESSING.

## LORD OF DEATH

A WILD PIG HAS DIED IN THE GRASSLANDS.
HE WAS ONCE AN INVASIVE SPECIES,
NOT NATIVE TO NORTH AMERICA,
BUT INTRODUCED BY EUROPEAN SETTLERS.
EVEN AS HE IS LYING DEAD IN FRONT OF ME,
I CAN STILL SEE HIS FEROCIOUS
NATURE.
THE THICK UNDERBRUSH IS FILLED WITH

MAGGOTS.
THERE'S NO SIGN OF INJURY,
JUST
DEATH.
MAYBE A SLIGHT BIT OF DECAY.
THERE WAS BEAUTY PRESENT
IN SILENCE.
AND AN INVOLUNTARY POWER OF

CONNECTION.
I FOUND MY CORPSE
AMONG ITS CORPSE.
NOT NATIVE,
BUT AN INVASIVE SPECIES
MYSELF,
WALTZING BETWEEN
HEAVEN AND HELL.

# ENTER THE KILL

IT'S THE FOURTH OF JULY
AND THE STREETS ARE
LOUD, BUSY WITH
CELEBRATION.
THERE'S A GOLDEN TEMPLE
ON THE HORIZON,
IT SITS ALMOST SUSPENDED
IN AIR,

AWAY FROM ALL FESTIVITIES.
IN IT IS THE VOICE OF SOLACE,
AND BEREAVEMENT, MARRED
BY CONSOLATION.
I ENTERED.
THERE ARE YOUTHFUL
PERSONAGES
WANDERING ABOUT,

AND MONKS.
THEY SPEAK TO ME REGARDING,
THE FOUR NOBLE TRUTHS,
AND THE NATURE OF SUFFERING.
THEY SAY, EVERYONE GOES
THROUGH IT. PAIN.
THEY SHOW ME ROSE INCENSE
AND TEACH ME TO MEDITATE.

IN MY MIND'S EYE I SEE A
CANOE.
IT'S ALONE IN ITS BEAUTY,
MOVING GRACEFULLY BY THE
WINDS THAT CARRY IT UPSTREAM.
I AM CONSCIOUS OF ITS
RURAL BEAUTY, SAD OF ITS NEGLECT,
YET PROUD OF ITS FIERCE VALOR.

## THE GALLOWS

A BODY HANGS FROM THE GALLOWS,
AND THE SPARKLING RIVER IN THE LANDSCAPE,
CAPTURES ITS REFLECTION,
DEEP WHERE THE SILENCE,
GROWS.
MANY WATCH CONTENTED,
FROM SANDY BEDS,
AND OPEN FIELDS.

THERE ARE NO MILD COURTESIES
HERE.
SOMETIMES I FEEL THIS IS HELL.
AND WE'RE TRAPPED IN SLOWLY
DECAYING BODIES AS PUNISHMENT.
WE GET TO SEE AND EXPERIENCE
OUR OWN DEATH.
AND OUR OWN ULTIMATE

SALVATION.
MANY OF MY BRETHREN,
KNOW THIS.
IT'S WRITTEN IN OUR SOULS,
AND OUR SOULS REMEMBER.
WE ARE THE CHOSEN ONES,
WITH SILKEN TRESSES, THAT WEAR
THE FATED CROWN.

## PURPLE POMP

THEY SAY THE COLOR PURPLE
IS SYMBOLIC OF ROYALTY. IT
GARNISHES THE FRILLS OF CAPES
DILIGENTLY, LIKE A PECULIARITY
WE'VE GROWN ACCUSTOMED
TO.
YOU CAN SEE IT AMONG
CHARITABLE
SOCIETIES.

AND IT IS OFTEN USED
FOR ANNIVERSARIES,
AND IN ACADEMIES
AND SCHOOLS,
ODES AND EXHIBITIONS.
I'VE SEEN IT TOO,
IN SKIN THAT HAS BEEN ABUSED,
IN BLOOD ONCE ITS

SETTLED.
I'VE SEEN IT IN BRUISES,
AND IN EYES SHUT BY
FISTS.
IT IS PREVALENT IN BIRTHMARKS,
AND UPON ONE'S DEATH.
I'VE SEEN IT IN CHILDREN,
AS THEY PLAY SPORTS.

IT'S THERE, IN THE POMP
AND CIRCUMSTANCES
OF LIFE AND DEATH. I'M NOT QUITE SURE
ABOUT ITS REGAL STATUS.
BUT IT'S THERE.
IN THE TAWDRY, DIRTY,
FINERY
OF EVERYDAY LIVING.

# THE SLIDING BOARD

THERE'S A MUSICAL SOCIETY,
THAT ALWAYS PUTS ON A
PRODUCTION, A REENACTMENT
OF THE PASSION OF CHRIST.
IT INVOLVES A PROCESSION
AND PLAY, THAT RECREATES
THE CRUCIFIXION OF  JESUS
CHRIST.

MY NEXT DOOR NEIGHBOR
USED TO CALL IT, THE CARAVAN
OF WOE.
AN INTERPRETATION I HAVE
ALWAYS FOUND TACTLESS.
TO ME THE SOUL'S BLOOD
CRIES OUT, AND I FEEL MY
CREATOR'S PAIN FROM THAT

FAR LAND TO MINE.
IT'S THE LINGERING VOICE
FROM ANCIENT CAVES,
FROM MOUNTAINS THAT LOOK
LIKE MONUMENTS, SEALED IN
SACRED TRUST, THAT SECURES
THE FAITH. LIKE
A CHILD'S SLIDING BOARD

YOU FEEL IN YOUR STOMACH
WHEN YOU DROP.
BEREAVEMENT IS A SACRED
THING. AND MANY, LIKE I,
CONSOLE OURSELVES THIS WAY.
IN SOLITUDE. WE OFFER NO
EXPLANATIONS FOR OUR BELIEFS,
TO THOSE WITH A ROCKY HEART.

# CRYSTAL OF A DREAM

LAST NIGHT I DREAMT
ABOUT THE RIVER,
THE WATER OF LIFE
SO PURE AND CLEAN
IN ITS BRILLIANCE
AND SUPERNATURAL
BEAUTY, THAT
IT IS ASSOCIATED

WITH THE DIVINE
AND THE SPIRIT
REALM.
IT IS SAID TO HAVE
BEEN FORMED BY
THE ELEMENTS OF
HEAVEN.
I QUIVERED AS I

BATHED IN IT.
FOR A MOMENT,
I STOOD STATIONARY,
FEELING THE RISING
SUN UPON MY FLESH.
THE CLOUDS, ROLLING
THEMSELVES UP LIKE
A SACRED TEXT.

WHITE LIGHT STREAMED
FROM THEM,
GLEAMED LIKE A
JAVELIN THROWN
WITH POWER.
I THOUGHT ABOUT
THE ALL SEEING EYE,
AND IMPLORED ITS
PERMISSION TO REMAIN.

## HOOKED AND ROPED

MY BEST FRIEND TOLD ME
TODAY, HE WAS BISEXUAL.
HE BEGGED ME TO UNDERSTAND
AS IF AFRAID TO BE SHUNNED.
HIS SOLICITATION SPOKE TO ME.
IN MY HEART HE WAS ALWAYS,
POETRY AMONG THE PEOPLE.
AND HE STILL IS.

HE'S IN HIS 60S NOW
BUT IS STILL A YOUTHFUL
PERSONAGE, POSSESSING ALL
THOSE INNER QUALITIES,
THAT MAKES A PERSON ATTRACTIVE.
PEOPLE HAVE HURT HIM,
THEN ASKED FOR FORGIVENESS.
HIS RESPONSE WAS ALWAYS

THE SAME.
"I FORGAVE YOU EVEN BEFORE
YOU ASKED."
HE WAS LOVING AND KIND,
EVEN WHEN JUDGED OR WRONGED.
HIS EYES ARE AN AMAZING BLUE,
AND HIS SMILE IS PORTRAIT WORTHY.
IN HIM, I SEE GOD, AND WITH HIM,

I SHALL STAY.
MY LOVE FOR HIM IS UNCONDITIONAL.
I SHALL CRUSH THE HEAD
OF ANY SERPENT,
THAT HAS HIM FEELING
UNWORTHY
OF THE SAME UNCONDITIONAL LOVE,
THAT GOD OFFERS HIM.

# STRANGLED INTO A SCREAM

THE SNAKE SLITHERS, ENTANGLES
ITSELF IN YOUR DREAMS,
BECKONS YOU TO DIALOGUE,
WEAVING YOU INTO ITS TRAP.
IT WILL HAUNT YOU VIA STARS SO
BRIGHT,
AND SACRIFICE YOU SUBLIME,
ON UPWARD PATHS OF PAIN


YOU'LL FIND YOURSELF,
GOING INSANE.
SO FAR AWAY, SEPARATE FROM
WONDROUS THOUGHTS, OF
GOD'S ETERNAL PLAN,
HE CAN UNDO WHAT HAS BEEN
DONE.
WHOSE SINS AM I TO BLAME?

I'VE SEEN TAPESTRIES COME TO
LIFE, RIGHT BEFORE MY EYES.
I'VE SEEN HATRED WEAVE ITS WEB,
WITH WAR'S ABHORRENT SIGHT.
AS SUNSETS FILL A DUSTY ROOM
WITH ITS BLOODY RED GLOW,
SHADOWS TURN TO SKIN AND BONE,
STRANGLED INTO A SCREAM,

AWAY FROM HOME. DEW FROM RAIN
BRINGS ABOUT HIS HOLY FACE,
LIKE A HEALING BALM OF OIL.
IT TRANS-SHIFTS ME FROM THE HORROR,
INTO ITS GROVE OF LILIES WHITE.
THERE ARE FRESH QUILTED COLORS
FLOATING THROUGH AIR, AND A BED
WHERE I CAN WEEP WITHOUT SORROW.

BITTER CRY

NATURE HAS ITS EMPTINESS TOO.
I'VE SEEN NUNS DEVOUT AND PURE
PLANT BERGAMOTS JUST TO WATCH
THEM DIE. EVEN THIS HIGHLY
ADAPTABLE PLANT WITH ITS SWEET
SMELL, TWINES WITH SUBTLE FEARS
AND HOPE THAT CANNOT SUSTAIN IT.
EVEN THROUGH ITS ADVENTUROUS


ESSENCE, THERE'S SOMETHING AMISS,
LIKE AN ADULTRESS WHO COMES TO REST
ON A FLAME, THEN DIES FROM THE BURN.
I WONDER IF ITS DEATH IS ITS BITTER
CRY,
OR IF THE FLOWER SIMPLY CANNOT THRIVE
IN THE ABSENCE OF LOVE.
I WONDER IF NATURE CAN TURN ON ITSELF,


BETRAY ITSELF, LIKE HUMAN BODIES DO.
THEY SAY THERE ARE NYMPHS THAT
PROTECT THE NATURAL WORLD.
THE DRYADS OF THE TREES,
THE NAIADS OF THE WATERS,
THE OREADS OF THE MOUNTAINS.
CAN THEY PLUCK THE THORNS AND DISARM?
I WONDER IF I CAN PROCURE VIOLETS,

MY FAVORITE FLOWER,
TO A LONGER AGE. DO I HAVE THAT POWER?
WITH IT I'D REFORM THE ERRORS
OF SPRING, AND SHARE THEM WITH
THE TULIPS.THIS IS WHAT SIMPLICITY
CAN BRING.
SWEETNESS.
THAT SEEMS FAIR.

## WILD REGRETS

WHILE STUDYING KABBALAH ONE NIGHT,
I SAW THE NEW MOON.
THE WIND WAS BLOWING THROUGH
THE TREES BUT THE MOON WAS UNAFFECTED.
I FELT ITS STRENGTH AND REALIZED
THE POWER IT HAD TO SWELL WAVES
AT ITS BECK AND CALL.
I FELT ITS RESILIENCE AND HOW IT

COULD PRESIDE OVER A BROKEN
SHIP, LIKE A JUDGE THAT DETERMINES
ITS FATE,
AND THE MEN IN SILKEN BLACK CLOTH,
AND THE LADIES WITH COVERED HAIR,
STAND INDESTRUCTIBLE,
IN UNISON WITH IT.
I'VE BEEN SHOWN THE PLAGUES

AND PULSES OF LIFE WITH THEM,
AND HAVE BEEN THE SINGING
CHANTICLEER WHILE READING THE SOLEMN
PAGES OF JEWISH PRACTICE AND THE PURPOSE
OF LIFE. I HAVE LAID SLEEPING IN THE
MOON'S EMBRACE,
APART FROM THE STARS AND BLOODY WARS.
APART FROM WILD REGRETS.

# CHAPEL OF THE DAY

STAINED GLASS WINDOWS,
IMPLORE LIGHT,
AND THERE'S BENEDICTINE CHANTS
THAT AWAKENS THE MIND.
I'VE ALWAYS LOVED ALL CHAPELS,
FROM THE MORE SIMPLISTIC ONES
ON RURAL ROADS, TO THE MORE
ORNATE.
AS RED CURTAINS BEGIN TO DRAW,

AND THE NIGHT SETTLES IN,
THE CHAPELS BECOME MORE OF A
HOME, A PLACE TO RETREAT TO.
A REWARD OF EQUAL GLORY
CROWNED.
CHAPEL DOORS SHOULD STAY
OPEN SO ALL THE WAYWARD
CAN ENTER AT ANY TIME.

THEIR CHAPEL FOR THE DAY,
THEIR HOME FOR THE NIGHT,
WHERE WEARINESS
CAN DROWN IN HOLY WATER
FONTS
AND BAPTISMAL BLESSINGS,
RENEWED ON
THE ALTAR.

HERE, GOD STANDS WITH
A WINGED SENTRY.
AND ARCHANGELS DESCEND
WITH FLOWERS OF PEACE.
IN THIS FORTRESS YOU ARE
SAFE
WITH THE LORD,
WITH YOUR LIFE, AND YOUR CURE.

## ONE MUST DIE

ONE MUST DIE THAT IS A CERTAINTY,
BUT THERE'S AN INDIGENOUS
VIEW OF ILLNESS.
THE DISEASE, A BREAKAGE,
A SEVERED CONNECTION
TO SOMETHING ONCE PRESENT,
NOW, COMPLETELY ABSENT.
THERE'S A PHYSICAL

MANIFESTATION TO SPIRITUAL
DECAY.
A DEATH THAT CROSSES MYSTICAL
PLANES.
AND SOULS THAT ACT AS INTERMEDIARIES,
AS A BRIDGE,
TO BRING US HOME.
SOMEONE INTONES A SONG,

AND MANY SING ALONG.
THE SPONTANEITY CAUSES MOST TO
BURST INTO TEARS WITH AUDIBLE
CRIES.
CEREMONIES, UNFORESEEN AND
UNPLANNED,
GIVE THE HUMAN SPIRIT PERMISSION
TO FLY. A RELEASE THROUGH FAMILIAR WORDS.

## WRITTEN IN HIS EYES

THERE ARE WATERS THAT SYMBOLIZE
A GATEWAY BETWEEN WORLDS,
ESPECIALLY WHEN DECORATED WITH
LIT CANDLES ALL ABOUT, INSPIRED TO
LOOK LIKE REFLECTIONS OF GLOWING
LIGHT, FLOATING WITH THEM.
THE ENTIRE SCENE EVOKES TRUST,
AND I STAND THERE, DOUBTFUL

AND LEERY. TRUST HAS NEVER COME
EASY FOR ME. IT HAS NEVER BEEN HEALING,
YET IN THIS PATH OF DANCING LIGHTS,
EVERYTHING SEEMS DYNAMIC, WORTHY
OF WARMTH AND BELIEF.
IF ONLY THIS FLUIDITY OF WATER,
BEAUTIFUL IN THE DARK,
WAS LIKE LIFE.


A PLACE WHERE TRUST ALIGNS
WITH VISION.
HOW DIFFERENT EVERYTHING WOULD
BE.
IT'S PAST MIDNIGHT AND I'M
TIRED.
I'M NOT RECEPTIVE ENOUGH TO
OPENNESS AT THE MOMENT.


THAT'S A CHALLENGE FOR ME.
PEOPLE ARE CRUEL, AND I'VE
RESPONDED TO THEM BY SHUTTING DOWN.
MY SAVIOR KNOWS THE PAIN OF ABUSE,
I'VE HAD TO DEAL WITH.
HOW I CARRY THE TRAUMA WITH ME.
IT IS WRITTEN IN MY EYES,
AND IN HIS EYES.

## TO LOOK UPON A WINE-RED ROSE

EARLY IN THE MORNING HOURS, I TOOK A WALK
ACROSS THE BEACH. THE SUN WAS STILL REDDISH-
ORANGE AND I COULD SEE FISH JUMPING IN
AND OUT OF THE WATER IN BOURBON RIPPLES.
THERE WERE SEASHELLS SCATTERED AND BURIED
IN THE SAND, AND AZALEA COLORED WAVES
THAT CRASHED TO SHORE.
THE AIR WAS SALTY, FRESH, AND I FELT GOOD.

A GRAY HAIRED WOMAN PAUSED IN THOUGHT,
WEARING A RED SWEATER WAS LOOKING OUT
INTO THE DEPTHS OF THE OCEAN.
WHEN I LOOKED UP, SHE JUST SEEMED TO
APPEAR THERE.
BLUE HAT ON HER HEAD,
AS IF GLUED TO A DREAM.
SHE DIDN'T MOVE AN INCH,

SHE JUST STOOD THERE STOIC,
HOLDING A WINE-RED ROSE IN HER HANDS.
I FELT LIKE I COULD GET INTO HER HEAD,
AND INVADE HER THOUGHTS.
SHE LOST SOMEONE.
SOMEONE SPECIAL.
MY HEART KNEW THIS.
HER MEMORY STIRRED,

AND I KEPT HER SECRET.
SHE NEVER REALIZED I COULD TOUCH HER,
HAD TOUCHED HER,
WITH MY OWN THOUGHTS
AND PRAYERS.
SHE NEVER REALIZED HER DEVOTION
HAD BECOME MY DEVOTION,
AMONG BIRD CALLS AND OPEN WATERS.

## UNHOLY GROUND

THERE ARE PEOPLE THAT FRIGHTEN ME.
THEY WALK ON UNHOLY GROUND,
THEY STEAL THE RADIANCE OF OTHERS,
JUST BECAUSE THEY CAN.
THEY ARE SHADOWS THAT DARKEN
SLEEPING BODIES, THEN DISCARD THEM
ON A PILE OF LEAVES, UNAFFECTED
AGAINST A BLACK SKY,

AGAINST A MASSIVE AUGMENT OF LIGHT;
THE TWO, FIGHTING FOR DOMINANCE,
YET STRANGE TO ONE ANOTHER.
WOUNDS CHURN IN WET GRASS,WHERE
SUFFERING IS ONLY AN APPEARANCE,
A GHOSTLY PRISONER LEFT ALONE AMONG
WILD BEASTS, JUST BEGINNING TO KNOW,
GOOD FROM EVIL.

IT'S NOT THE MOON THAT HUMILIATES,
WHERE CRIES ESCAPE IN PURRING
SOUNDS, THAT MOUNT AND SPIT WHERE
FOOLS ARE MADE OF.
IT'S NOT THE FOUL ODORS OR THE PARALYZING
SOULS THAT SEEK FORGIVENESS AMONG
DEAD FLIES ON THY FATHER'S BED, NOR
THE SEARING KISSES ON ONE'S FOREHEAD

THAT STOKES YOU GENTLY AWAKE.
IT'S THE MOURNING OF THE LAST TIME
IN HIS PRESENCE, WHERE THE SUN IS COLD
AND YOU WITH FLUSHED FACE REALIZE
THE CONTRACT HAS BEEN SEALED, THAT
KILLS YOU. IT'S THE LACK OF LOVE AND GRACE,
THAT COMMITS YOU TO SILENCE, AND
SENTENCES YOU INTO THE HANDS OF THE IMPOSTER.

## BRITTLE BONE BY NIGHT

THE POOR IN SPIRIT ARE BRITTLE BONE
BY NIGHT, AND WANDER IN THE ABSTRACT,
LIKE A PAINTING WITHOUT PURPOSE OR
MEANING. THEIR COLORS ARE AN INTENSE
SHADE OF ECSTATIC DISREGARD THAT RUSHES
FORWARD AT YOUR EYES WITHOUT SUSTENANCE,
SLIGHTLY DEEPENING TO THE OFTEN CONFUSED
RESPONSES OF THOSE THAT WATCH, STIMULATED

BY DESPAIR. MANY GET TO REVEL IN THEIR
NATURE, FROM AFAR, AS THEY CLIMB THE
WALLS OF THEOLOGICAL GIFTS NOT GIVEN,
BUT PRESERVED BY THE ADVANTAGE OF
ILLUSIONS. WAX CANDLES DRIP FROM THEIR
LIQUIFIED EMBANKMENTS, AS IF RECITING A
PRAYER OF REMEMBRANCE, WHERE BELLS TOLL ON
THE HOUR AND WILD HAWTHORN SWAYS

UNATTENDED BY SEEING EYES. AMONG THE MOST
VALUABLE IS THE GRIEF THAT BINDS YOU TO EARTH,
THE CLINGING OF BURNING FIELDS ALL AROUND, THAT
SIMPLY WON'T LET YOU GO. THE FEAR IN DEATH
SO COMMUNAL, PUNISHMENT IS BEYOND ITS OWN
CREATION. IN THIS STATE THE SLENDER BRANCHES OF
TREES, SHIFT AND RUSTLE, LIKE RATTLING BONES AT
NIGHT, BEARING NO SIGN OF LIFE WHATSOEVER.

# WONDERING SKY

IT'S WHAT YOU FEAR THE MOST THAT CALLS OUT
TO YOU. A VOICE THAT DRIFTS IN ECHOES
ABSORBED INTO THE DARKNESS, WITH NOTHING
BUT BLACKNESS BEHIND IT. IT'S THE WONDERING
SKY THAT HAS YOU DRAWN, SOMEWHERE BETWEEN
SEAS AND MOUNTAINS. THERE ARE YOUNG CHILDREN
WAITING FOR A STORY TO BE WRITTEN AND THEY LIVE
INSIDE OUR HEARTS.

THEIR PENS ARE MADE OF BOLDNESS AND PASSION,
CONFIDENT NOT TO HAVE LIVED THE TRAGEDIES
THAT WILL SOMEDAY MARK THEIR LIVES. THEY DREAM
BY OPEN WINDOWS, IN SUMMER MORNINGS OF
YELLOWISH—WHITE, WITH PETALS ON SCREENS, THEY
SCRIBBLE WORDS ABOUT THE FIRST RAINS OF AUTUMN,
AND RIPEN PUMPKINS 30 IMPERIAL, THEY BREATHE
WITH FLARE ON THEIR OWN.

WE WERE ONCE THEM, GATHERED TOGETHER IN
NIGHTS THAT GREW WARM THEN COOL IN THE SILENCE.
WE HOWLED AT THE FULL MOON, DANCED WITH THE
NEW MOON, AND WISHED FOR SNOWDROPS AND GUMDROPS
WITH THE HALF—MOON.
MAPLES MAY FALL IN GENTLE DRIPS, AND A SOFT NEON SILVER
CAN DISPENSE WITH THE CHAOS, SUMMONING INTO
EXISTENCE EVERY MONSTER AND DEMON AROUND,

COMPANIONS, FADING IN TWILIGHT. BETWEEN THEM, A
BED OF INVISIBLE STARS, OBSCURED BY THE MISTS AND FOG
THAT BLINDS US, YET LINGERS ON IN THE HORIZON THROUGH
UNSCENTED AIR. A CHURNING OF EVIL ENTRAPS WITHIN
THE SPLENDOR OF AN ENTERED ETERNITY. WHERE MUSIC IS
NON EXISTENT, AND POEMS GRAB YOU BY TROUBLESOME WATERS
IMPLICITLY TRANSFORMED FOREVER. THIS IS WHERE IT ALL VANISH—
ES,
WITHOUT A VOICE, INTO AN IMPASSIVE PROCESS.

## A BLOOM IN PRISON AIR

NYMPHS DON'T APPEAR AS BLOOMS IN PRISON
AIR. THEIR SOULS CAN'T GRAZE WHERE HANDS
HAVE NOT TOUCHED, AND WHAT THEY RECALL
OF THE UNDERWORLD IS SUBJECT TO CENSURE.
THEY DON'T GRANT WISHES VIA MAGIC CRYSTALS,
EVEN WHEN UNDERSTOOD THAT THEY BELONG TO
YOU. AND SCEPTERS ARE BORN OF APHRODITE,
NOT VENUS, AND LOVE HAS ITS OWN REASONING.

THERE'S THE AUSTERITY OF BALANCE THAT HANGS
THE SCALES OF JUSTICE, AND I ASK MYSELF, "WHO
HAS ARRANGED ALL THIS?" AND I RECOGNIZE THE
FALLEN IN THE EXACTITIES OF REASONING, HOW MUCH
IS LOST AND DESTROYED AS THE RESULT OF ACTION.
THE SMELL OF SMOKE SUFFOCATES, BURNS FLESH
TOO STUBBORN TO DIE.
AND THE WORLD CHANGES, AND NOT FOR THE BETTER.

WE ARE NOT RAISED TO A HIGHER POWER, AND THE
SEPARATION OF TREES IS A TERRIBLE THING, AND MUSIC
CONTINUES WITHOUT INSTRUMENTS, LIKE AN IDEA
FOUND ONLY IN A DREAM. THERE ARE DOVES THAT RISE,
GLOWING IN THE SUNSET, AND THAT'S ENOUGH TO SAY
GOODBYE FOREVER. AND SOME THINK IT BEAUTIFUL
AND PROFOUNDLY TENDER WHILE OTHERS THINK IT

CRUEL.
THERE'S UNSPEAKABLE TENDERNESS IN RADIANT WATERS,
AND IN THE WORD AS IS. I BELIEVE THAT SPLITS THE ROADS
IN TWO, PREEMPTIVE OF WHAT'S TO COME.
NIGHT'S ARE METICULOUS IN THEIR MYSTERY AS SHEETS
OF ICE RISE IN SMALL INCREMENTS.
BODIES AGE AND TIME WILL RAVAGE YOU, SUBLIME,
INDIFFERENT, WITH NEVER A WORD OF CAUTION TO PROTECT YOU.

## CANVAS ON CLOTHES

MORNING DOZES AND SHADOWS RISE UP
FROM SODDEN DITCHES. THERE'S A MILD
HARROWING BREEZE AND CHILDREN ARE
LATE FOR SCHOOL. THEIR UNIFORMS, LIKE
CANVAS ON CLOTHES, NOT ALWAYS A
TRANSPARENT PAGE, BUT HELD FIRMLY
STORYBOUND BY THEIR PLACE IN THE DUSK.
IMAGES IN ANOTHER PALLET TWEAK WITH

WHITE BLOSSOMS AND SPEAK OF ORCHARDS
WAY OUT OF REACH. AMMUNITION FOR THOSE
WHO LOVE A CHALLENGE AND VIEW LIFE AS AN
ADVENTURE. IN DEEP GROVES THE BREATH
OF ASHES FLOWS LIKE A RIVER, AS SOOT THICKENS
ALL AROUND. THERE ARE WAVES OF GOODWILL
AND CHARITY THAT EXTENDS ALONGSIDE A
BEDSIDE OF ROSES, NEVER TO BE TOUCHED.

HALF—LIGHT AND STONE HOUSES CAN SOMETIMES
BE IDENTICAL, HOLLOWED WITH ECHOES THAT
SCREAM, TOUCH ME NOW, AMONG TENDER
UNDERTHINGS THAT CLOUD ONE'S JUDGEMENT,
AS THEY INSTRUCT YOU IN THE DARK.
THE DEAD ARE STIRRED, AND THE PLEIADES
CAN BE SEEN FROM THE TOMBS, AS IT PASSES
INTO STATIONARY DARKNESS.

THE BLIND AND THE WEIGHTLESS WHISTLE,
SIFTING THE WATERS OVER PONDS; BLUE
LACKLUSTER AND PERMANENT. AND THE WILLOWS,
THEY STRETCH OUT AMONG MIRRORED MOONS,
THEIR ENERGY COMPLEX AND IMPENETRABLE.
THE WILDLIFE IS ROUGHHOUSING, AWAY FROM
THE WORLD, IN THE DISTANCE LIKE A PAINTING
COME TO LIFE, WITHOUT A SOUL. WITHOUT CONTEXT.

## THE STARTLED SOUL

THE MOON IS NAKED AND THE MISTS
HAVE UNCOVERED IT, UNDRESSED IT,
LIKE A STARTLED SOUL IN THE NIGHT
SKY. THE RAIN HAS BEGUN AND THE
NEW YORK CITY STREET CARS ARE COVERED
WITH DROPLETS THAT RESEMBLE TEARS.
IT'S THAT SOFT KIND OF RAIN, SWEET AS
EARTH, THAT GIVES SHADOW TO DUSK,

DARK BODIES IN ITS WAKE. AND THAT
YELLOW GLOW THAT SCATTERS, SMELLS
LIKE URINE, AND LEAVES YOU FEELING
LIKE SOMETHING IS WRONG WITH THE UNIVERSE.
I WALK VIA MARBLE AND STONE, AND CENTURIES
OLD MOONLIGHT QUIET FOR MORE THAN A
MILLION YEARS. I WONDER ABOUT TIME,
AND WHERE GOD IS, WITH EVERY GOLDEN,

SWIFT HOUR THAT PASSES BY. IT IS TO ME A
PRAYER, SINFUL IN HAPPINESS, AND DANCING
IN THE SUNSHINE, AND DREAMING OF LOVE,
AND OTHER USELESS THINGS. THE GRAVEYARDS
ARE BLUE WITH IT, OVER GREEN MOSS ATTACHED
SO THICK, YOU CAN'T READ THE NAMES. A ROSE
WHOSE BREATH IS SWEET, BREAKS AND DIES
IN ERODED AIR. A CURSE REBORN INTO SOMETHING

GENERATIONAL. IT FOLLOWS, AND YOU KNOW IT
WILL COME AGAIN, SAVE THE BEAT BACK INTO THE
BLOOD. AND THE DRUMS, THEY COMMAND ME
TO UNDERSTAND, OF THE BITTER YEARNINGS LOST,
AND LEFT UNWRITTEN. DESIRE AND DREAMS SPIT
IN YOUR FACE, AND WITH FISTS CLENCHED YOU TAKE
THE HIT, UNTIL THE LAST MOLECULE, IS NO MOLECULE
AT ALL.

# THE VILEST DEEDS

THEY DON'T TELL YOU THAT SOME
MEDICATIONS CAN KILL YOU FASTER
THAN THE DISEASE. AND THEY DON'T
TELL YOU THAT MEDICAL TESTS AREN'T
ALWAYS ACCURATE OR THAT THE GOVERNMENT
WILL NOT TAKE CARE OF YOU WHEN
YOU'RE OLD AND SICK. NO ONE TELLS YOU
THAT DREAMS CAN COME WITH CRUEL


CONSEQUENCES, AND BITTERNESS REMAINS,
NEVER RESOLVING ITSELF. AND NO WILL
EVER CONFESSES HOW FAST TIME FLIES,
AND HOW THE CHILDHOOD NEIGHBORHOOD
YOU ONCE LOVED CHANGED TO A PLACE
THAT'S UNRECOGNIZABLE. AND HOW YOUR
FRIENDS MOVED FAR AWAY LITTLE BY LITTLE,
BEFORE THEY DIED.

NO ONE LIKES TO SPEAK OF ENDINGS AND DEATH,
AND WHY GOD PUTS US THROUGH THAT, AND HOW
THE TORCHES WE CARRY FOR TOMORROW WILL
EVENTUALLY BLOW OUT. NO TALKS ABOUT
THE PAST ROADS TO THE LIGHT OR THE IGNORANCE
THEY FELT IN THE STRUGGLE AND STRIFE.
NO ONE DARES TO STAND WITH THE BIBLE IN HAND
FEELING DEATH CREEP, AS LIVES BURN IN THE DARK.

AND HOW THE VILEST OF DEEDS COME WITH THE
BEST OF INTENTIONS, OR HOW TWIN TOWERS CAN FALL
BY AN EVIL PERSON'S HANDS. THE CLOCK TICKS
RENDERING YOU HELPLESS AS IT PLOWS AGAINST
SCATTERED EARTH. IT WILL CRUSH THE MIGHTY,
MAKING SERVANTS OF US ALL, AS IT CALLS OUR
HOMELAND FREE, BORN OF SWEAT AND BLOOD,
WHOSE FAITH BEQUEATHS PAIN, WE CAN SEE.

## LAWS BE RIGHT

CHURCHES AND SCHOOLS ARE CLOSING FOR GOOD,
WHILE THE RISING POWER OF OUR VOTES THAT
HELPED BUILD A DEMOCRACY CRASHES.
ALL ILLUSIONS FED TO US, WOVEN IN CONTROL.
IF LAWS BE RIGHT, WHY ARE GREAT NATIONS
CRUMBLING, AND CHILDREN WITH CANCER DEPORTED?
CONSIDER US THEM. WE SEE GRAND MARSHAL'S
IN SUITS WITH DIGNITARIES IN LIMOS AND MOTOR–CADES


OF SOLID BLACK. THEY PARADE WHAT SELLS IN THE
GUISE OF LIBERTY AND JUSTICE, THEN BLAME US
WHEN THEY FALL. IF GOD WERE A WOMAN WOULD
LAWS BE RIGHT? WOULD WORKING TO THE BONE
MEAN NOTHING AT ALL? WHEN THE CLOCK STRIKES
TWELVE AND NEON LIGHTS MAKE A CROWN, AND THERE'S
NO MONEY TO PAY THE BILLS, WOULD WE STAND AND
LISTEN TO IT PLAY?

I WAS BORN HERE BENEATH GOD'S SKY, AND CRADLED
IN HIS ARMS. IF LAWS BE RIGHT AM I ONE OF THE
DISPLACED? ONE OF THE SHIRTLESS? IF MONEY
ROLLED IN AND BLOOD RAN OUT WOULD THAT MAKE
ME A BETTER PERSON? DOES CLOUT SETTLE ACHING
HEARTS AND TELL THE TRUTH OF SURRENDER? WHEN MY
LANDLORD HANDS ME EVICTION PAPERS, AND I'M
THROWN AWAY ON THE STREETS, WILL LAWS BE RIGHT?

I WANT TO KNOW IF I'M TETHERED BY SOMETHING
WORSE THAN PRIDE, AND IF IT WILL BE LIKE A DRUG THAT
KILLS ME. I WANT TO KNOW HOW EXPENDABLE I AM
IN YOUR EYES, DEAR SAVIOR, AND WHY MY BEAUTY
HAS TO MELT LIKE SNOW FOR YOU TO HEAR ME.
I WANT TO KNOW IF YOU WILL TAKE ME FROM THE CRAZINESS,
AND TELL ME EVERYTHING'S GOING TO BE ALRIGHT.
I WANT TO KNOW IF YOU'VE GOT ME, LORD!

## OUTCASTS ALWAYS MOURN

I RIDE THE WAVES OF DEEP—BLUE SEAWATER,
AND BURY MY FEET IN WET SAND. THERE
ARE OBJECTS ON THE OCEAN FLOATING
WITH SEAWEED, AND I'M OBSERVANT OF THE
DETAILS. THE GREAT DIFFICULTIES OF LIFE
DON'T EXIST HERE AMONG NATURAL FORCES,
UNIMAGINABLE. THE NIGHTS AREN'T AS DARK
AS YOU WOULD THINK, EVEN WHEN THEY

STAY WITH ME A LITTLE LONGER. THE LIGHTHOUSE
I SEE, KEEPS ME AWAKE, AND THE ROCKS SHINE
BRIGHT WITH SALTY SLIME. AND THE SPELLS I CAST
MEET THE RIPPLES UPON THE SEA AS MOTION
MEETS TIME. BREEZES BLOWN GENTLY,
SEND IT ON ITS WAY, AND THE GODDESS STEEPED
IN SADNESS CRIES OUT FOR ONE MORE DAY.
AND ANGELS SING OUT BENEATH THE FLOW,

OF SULPHUROUS STARS SO BRIGHT THEY GLOW.
I WONDER WHERE THEY FELL FROM; OUTCASTS
OF THE NIGHT. DRUMBEATS LINE THE COASTLINE,
IN THE SIGHT OF AN APPROACHING STORM.
THERE'S DAZZLING IMMORTALITY IN THE WAY THAT
IT FORMS.I RETURN BACK TO SHORE AND LOOK BEHIND
ME BY SLOW DEGREES, AND THERE IT STILL STANDS
THE SEA AMONG THE SEAS.

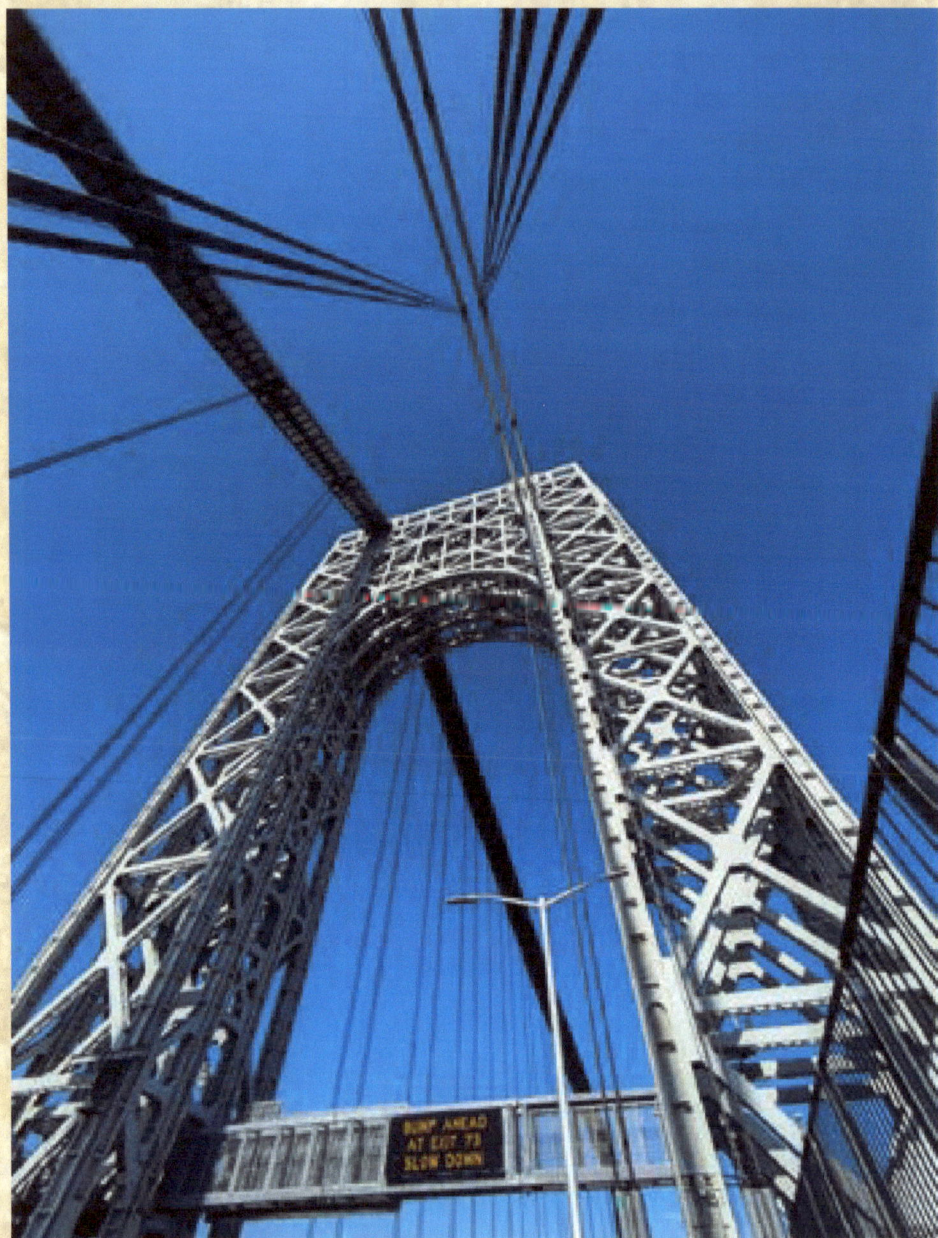

# MEN BUILT OF SHAME

THEY STOOD SIDE BY SIDE LIKE WOODEN
SOLDIERS, SMALL AND SLY WITH GOD. WICKED
MEN WITH WICKED MINDS A METAPHOR PATCH
TO COVER ONE EYE. THEY WHISPERED NEWS
TO WOODEN EARS AND MANY BELIEVED THEIR
LIES, AS BIG BLACK CLOUDS ROLLED FIRMLY ACROSS
THE SKIES. THEIR EYES SEARCHED THE ROOM
FOR THOSE HUNGRY FOR GLEAMING JEWELS,


AND ALL WHO PARTOOK WERE NOTHING MORE THAN
A BUNCH OF THIRSTY FOOLS. I WONDER WHEN THE
STARS WILL FALL AND WHEN THEY WILL GROW DIM. I
WONDER IF THE EARTH WILL BECOME COLD AND IF WE'LL
LOSE OUR KIN.
IF CLIMATE CHANGE IS REAL WILL IT GO ON TO
BE IGNORED? WILL WE LOOK UPON A CAGE ONE DAY AND
SEE NOTHING TO BE STORED?

## THEY SCOURGE THE STRONG

THE ANGEL OF DEATH FLIES OVERHEAD TONIGHT.
I HAVE FELT ITS PRESENCE PRIOR TO, IMPARTIAL,
WEIGHING THE HEADS BEFORE IT, EXAMINING
THE DEEDS DONE DIRTY AND CLEAN, TRACING THE
SCALES OF JUSTICE WITH ITS FINGERS. THERE'S A
RESIDUE THAT REMAINS LIKE THE FRAGMENTS OF
POETRY WRITTEN ABOUT IT DAILY, IN THE HEAT OF
PAVEMENTS WALKED ON AND THE FLAME OF THE

SUN. NOTHING IS FIXED IN THE FOUNTAINS OF CREATION,
AND THERE IS NO REAL ASSURANCE OF DEATH. IF
EARTH CAN SPRING BACK TO LIFE, THEN SO CAN WE,
EVEN IF VICTIMS OF DESTINY. THERE'S A PART OF ME
THAT'S PARALYZED WITH FEAR AND A PART OF ME THAT
FEELS SAFE AND SECURE. I CAN BE TOUCHED AND NOT
BE REJECTED WITHIN THE SPLENDOR OF ALL WILD THINGS
UNEXPLORED.

I CAN DISCONNECT FROM MY LIMBS AND DISSOLVE
INTO BOUNDLESS AIR, WITHOUT BELONGING TO ANY DREAM,
LOST IN THE ENERGY OF ETERNITY. IF I EVER BECOME A
MODEL FOR STRUCTURE, THAT MAY BE AN ASSUMPTION
MADE ON YOUR PART, AS I TRAVEL EVERYWHERE IN
WAVES, AMONG HIGH TRESTLES AND COMMON KINDNESS,
KNOWING THE PEAKS OF OBLIVION CURE ME, AND NO
ONE ASKS FOR ME, ANYMORE.

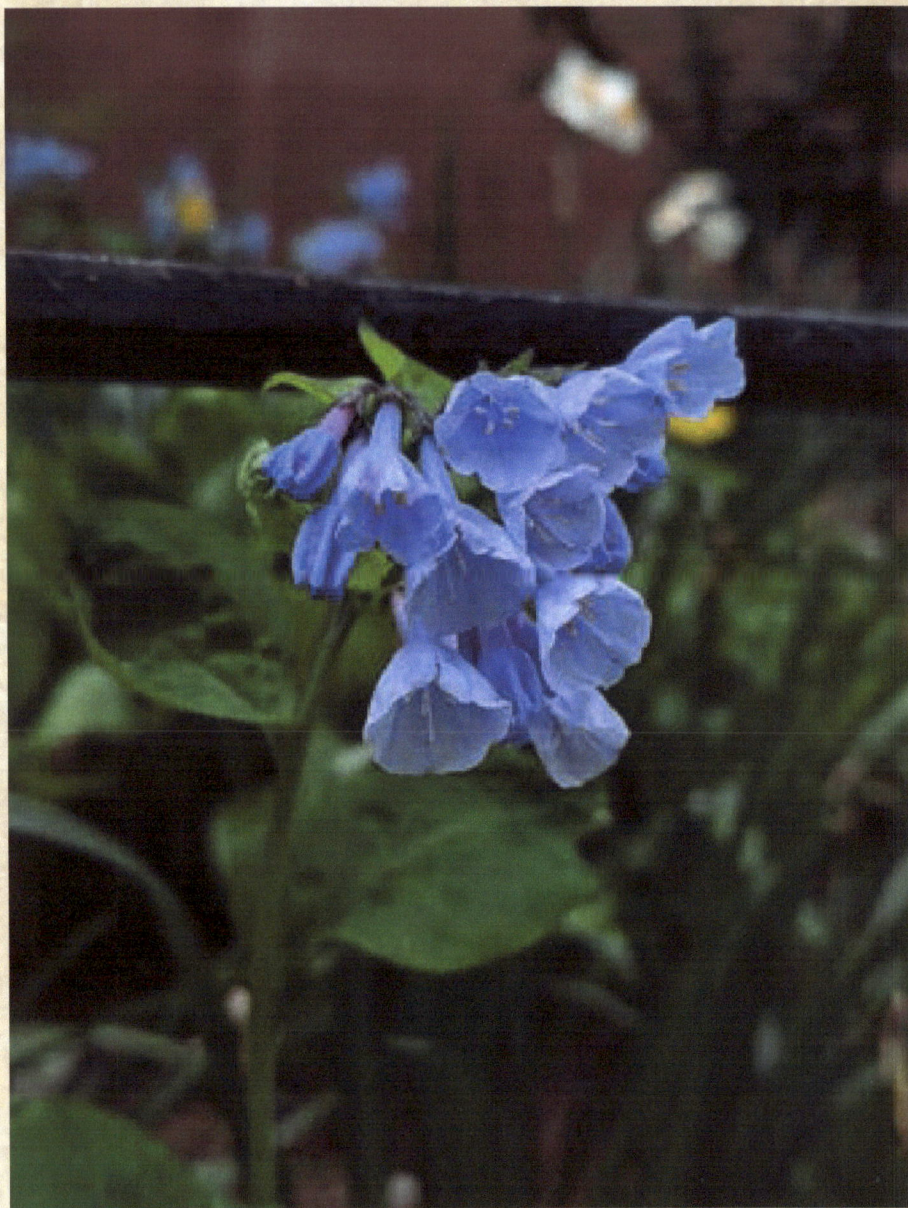

## OLD AND GREY

IT HAPPENED ONCE, AT A TIME
WHEN I DISLIKED PEOPLE
AND WANTED NO FRIENDS.
I TOOK A WALK OVER A LARGE
BRIDGE, INTO A FIELD OF  BLUE
FLOWERS. THEY HUNG LIKE
BELLS STARING DOWN AWAY FROM
MY GAZE. PERHAPS THE FLOWERS


DIDN'T WANT ANY FRIENDS
EITHER. NO EMOTIONAL ATTACHMENTS
TO ANYTHING AROUND IT NOR IN
FRONT OF IT. I GUESS IT HAD BEEN
IN A PLACE OF NO LIGHT, EVEN THOUGH
THE SUN BEAT DOWN UPON IT WITH FULL
FORCE. PERHAPS IT WAS WEEPING,
MOURNING SOME KIND OF LOSS, INEXPLICABLE.

I SAW ITS WILTED FACE AND EXAMINED
ITS BROKEN STEM. AND I THOUGHT,
IT MAY HAVE TRUSTED, WHEN IT SHOULDN'T.
AND IN THE WILD HOT MOONS OF SUMMER,
BROKEN —WINGED BIRDS THAT CANNOT FLY
SETTLE DOWN AMONG THEM, OLD AND GREY,
SEEKING HEAVY SHADE. AND WELL, THE EYES
OF THE PEOPLE, THEY JUST LOOK AWAY.

# THE FETID BREATH OF DEATH

AS I WATCH THE CRESCENT MOON
AND THE NIGHT GROWS DARK,
I THINK ABOUT THE WAY SPRING
STRETCHES ABOVE FLOWERS. THE EARTH
ENDS THEN BEGINS AGAIN AND AGAIN,
AND BECKONS ITS SEEDS TO DO THE
SAME. THERE'S SOMETHING SO DELICATE
ABOUT THE POSSIBILITY OF REBIRTH,

AND HOW JESUS WAS SUBJECT TO BE
FINISHED, BUT WAS BROUGHT BACK TO
LIFE. I THOUGHT ABOUT HOW MANY TIMES
I DIED, HOW MANY TIMES I WAS DROPPED
BY THE WORLD, DISCARDED LIKE TRASH,
ONLY TO RISE AGAIN. IT HAPPENS BY
SHEER WILL, THE RISING, AND BY EARTH'S
MAGIC.

THE REGENERATION IS UNIQUE TO THE INDIVIDUAL,
TO THE MIND INVISIBLE NO ONE CAN SEE
NOR UNDERSTAND. THERE'S A BEAUTIFUL NEW
BODY, IDENTICAL TO ITS MIND, CONSISTENT
WITH HOW GOD HAS MADE US. WE'RE
DELICATE, FRAGILE, AND WITH LOTS OF LOVE
AND CARE, WE START TO POKE OUT OF THE DIRT,
AWAY FROM THE FETID BREATH OF DEATH.

# BRACKISH WATER

BRACKISH WATER ABSTRACT, PUDDLES
AROUND IN YOUR GARDEN. THERE'S
A SMALL HILL ABOVE WILD BLUEBERRIES,
THAT DESCENDS INTO A DEEP ABYSS. I
SOMETIMES PEER INTO IT FROM ABOVE,
INTO THE DARKNESS. THE PHYSICAL WORLD
THAT SURROUNDS IT, CONTRIBUTES TO THE
SILENCE.

A PUTRID SMELL EMANATES FROM THAT
DEEP ABYSS, A MIXTURE OF WAX AND
DEATH, AND ROTTEN FRUITS, BEYOND
THE NATURAL SWEET SMELLS IT HIDES.
THERE ARE MOMENTS WHEN ITS ENERGY
WASHES OVER ME AND IT LEAVES ME HURTING,
LIKE A BARE TREE, EXPOSED FOR ALL TO SEE,
ONLY I'M ALONE WITH MYSELF, IN SPITE OF

MYSELF AND BECAUSE OF MYSELF. I HOLD
NO VALUE, AND THAT TURNS OTHERS AWAY,
SEPARATE FROM ME. MOST OF THE TIME I
RESEMBLE COMPLETE DETACHMENT, AS I
FIGHT THE DEMONS FROM WITHIN. I STRUGGLE
TO ACHIEVE, TO PERFECT MYSELF AND ALL THINGS,
YET I SOMETIMES FAIL. I'M NOT POWERFUL
ENOUGH TO TURN BRACKISH WATER CLEAN.

## THE LOVELIEST OF TREES


BENEATH THE ELM I FEEL HIS PROTECTION,
AMONG SCENTS OF EARTH AND FLOWERS
THAT TAKE AWAY MY BREATH. THE SUN BRANDS
ME WITH COLOR, AND THE SHADOWS OF BIRDS
CIRCLE ABOVE ME. I DREAM OF HIS RETURN.
IT PARADES INSIDE MY HEAD OFTEN. I SEE
MYSELF BY HIS SIDE, THE GROUND STIRRING
BENEATH US.

HE TOUCHES ME WITH HIS LOVE, IT'S
UNCONDITIONAL AND PURE. HE CLEANSES
ME OF MY SINS, AND I TRUST IN HIM
COMPLETELY AND OPENLY CONFESS. HE'S
HONESTY AND MOON DROPS, SUNKISSED WITH
LIGHT, AND HE SHOWS ME THERE'S A SPECIAL
GIFT WAITING FOR ME ON THE OTHER SIDE.
HE GUIDES ME TO A FIELD AND SUMMONS FORTH

A CREATURE. IT GENTLY COMES OVER TO HIM
AND I RECOGNIZE IT AS ONE OF MY FURBABIES,
MY DOT. THE KITTY RECOGNIZES ME TOO AND
I RUN TO HER IN TEARS YELLING HER NAME IN
JOY. THIS IS WHEN I WAKE UP. THIS IS WHERE
PONDS BETWEEN MOUNTAINS THROB FROM
THE HEAT OF THE SUN AND WHERE PROMISES ARE
KEPT AMONG THE LOVELIEST OF TREES.

## ALONG THE BOUGH

SNOW SETTLES ALONG THE BOUGH
AND THE SMELL OF PINE IS
INTOXICATING. THEY ARE KNOWN
FOR THEIR LONGEVITY AND RESILIENCE.
THEY ARE BEAUTIFUL AND ENDURE
MUCH HARDSHIP. THEY ARE WISE,
AND PROTECT, HEAL AND PURIFY.
THEY ARE SIMPLE, LIKE THE PINE


CASKETS MADE FROM THEIR WOOD.
JESUS DANCES UNDER THEM AND THE
HOLY SPIRIT IMPARTS THEM WITH ITS
GIFTS, WHILE GOD WATCHES FROM
ABOVE.
BLUE SPRUCES STARE AT THEM WITH
WONDER, A PASSIONATE ONSET TO
THE STRIKING MAGNIFICENCE BEFORE


THEM. I RUN BAREFOOTED AROUND THE
PINES, AND GET DIZZY, LIKE A CHILD,
WITH ENTHUSIASM BLURRED AND
DISFIGURED. I FEEL THE WIND SWEEP
AGAINST MY FEET, AND THE STICKS
AND STONES COVER MY TOES WITH
DISPLACED EARTH. I SEE THE DESOLATION
OF NOVEMBER, AND THE JOY OF DECEMBER!

WOODLAND RIDE

ROWBOATS CAN BE A WOODLAND RIDE
ALONG GREEN, VIOLET AND RED SHORES,
A CARGO FULL OF LUSH LANDS THAT SMELL
OF SANDALWOOD. IT'S A VERY DISTINCT
SCENT, SPECIAL AND UNIQUE, THE WAY
GOD MADE IT, THE WAY HE INTENDED
IT TO BE. AND THE LAKE, HAS NOT
DISAPPOINTED EITHER, WITH ITS MEASURED


RIPPLES OF PLEASANT WAVES THAT ROCK
ME GENTLY BACK AND FORTH. I WONDER
IF THIS WAS HIS DESIGN ALL ALONG. IF
THIS IS HOW HE CONNECTS WITH US,
HEALS US FROM DESPAIR AND SKEPTICISM.
I OFTEN WONDER IF THE NORTH WIND WILL
EVER GET TIRED AND IF I'LL EVER STOP
HEARING THE SWEETNESS OF SOFT RAIN,


FALL METICULOUSLY UPON MY ROOF.
NATURE IS MY REPOSE AND MY RESPITE,
AND THE BIRD'S SONGS AND VOICES,
MY COMPANIONS, MY BEST FRIENDS,
ESPECIALLY WHEN ANXIETY AND DOUBT
SET IN OR WHEN I'VE JUST BEEN BETRAYED
BY SOMEONE I LOVED AND TRUSTED.
I SPEAK TO HIM UNDER THE STARS AT NIGHT,

AND IN THE MIDNIGHT WALKS I TAKE.
I CAN SLEEP UPON THE WATERS, THEY BRING
ME WHITE PEACE. SOMETIMES I FEEL LIKE
AN ANCIENT SACRIFICE, OR SOME OLD
CATASTROPHE WAITING TO REPEAT ITSELF.
AND SOMETIMES, AMONG WATERED—LIGHTS,
I FEEL WILD AND FREE, LIKE THE WINDING
PATHS NEAR CALM WATERS, WITHOUT SOUND.

## CHERRY HUNG WITH SNOW

THE ELDERLY HAVE NO DIGNITY IN THIS WORLD.
IT HAS BEEN STRIPPED FROM US, BY THOSE
WHO VIEW US AS USELESS. I TAKE MY PLACE
UPON DISCARDED THINGS, AND REMEMBER
WHEN I WAS THE WHITE BLOSSOM OF THE
CHERRY TREE. GOD ALLOWS THIS PROCESS
TO REMIND US HOW FLEETING IT ALL IS,
AND HOW FIELDS OF PRAISE CAN ONE DAY TURN

BARREN, INTO HIGH FIELDS OF GREEN AND
DYING. NO ONE GIVES A DAMN AND MOST
DO THINGS OUT OF OBLIGATION. NEVER
FEELING MUCH, EITHER BY FEAR OR PURE, RAW,
NATURE. MANY BLASPHEME DOWN DEEP
UPON THEIR BREATH, WHILE GIVING ELEGIES
OF INNOCENCE AND YOUTH.
AS LOVE DRIPS AND GATHERS LIKE A VAMPIRE

ON A PSYCHIC ATTACK. TODAY, I'M EASED
BY SUMMER DAYS, AND GARDENS FILLED
WITH LADYBUGS AND BEES. TOMORROW, I
WILL GO BACKWARDS AND FORWARD, SILENT
IN MY CONFUSION, AND SICK FROM THE
CONFLICT.
THERE ARE HEADSTONES I VISIT, EMPTY
WITH ABANDONMENT, AND RUMORS OF

IMMORTALITY. I FEEL FOR THEM AND FOR THE
BODIES BURIED THERE, FORGOTTEN. I WONDER
IF THEY ONCE ADMIRED TALL SHIPS AND LET
THE OCEANS TAKE THEIR SOULS AWAY. I WONDER
IF THEY LOVED LEMON MERINGUE PIE AND
WHIPPED CREAM AND IF THEY EVER ROASTED
MARSHMALLOWS ON AN OPEN FIRE, AND DID THEY
EVER ADMIRE A CHERRY TREE HUNG WITH SNOW.

## LIGHTFOOT LAND

I HEAR THE VOICES OF THE INDIGENOUS
PEOPLE. THEY COME WITH SHOOTING
STARS BY MOONLIGHT. I REALIZE THE
PATTERNS OF THEIR DRUM BEATS,
AND THAT OF THEIR ARRIVAL. THERE
ARE DIM SHAPES OF WOMEN STOOPING
DOWN BEHIND BUSHES IN THE WILD AND
CREEPING SLOWLY FORMING SHADOWS.

THE LAND SHELTERS THEM BY COLD WATERS,
AND THEY SLEEP THERE BY FLOWERS WHOSE
COLORS NEVER FADE. ON THEIR KNEES,
THEY LEAVE OFFERINGS TO THE GREAT SPIRIT
BY THE RIVER'S EDGE AND PLACE MAZE AND
WARM BREAD UNDER TREES FOUND IN THE
FOREST, FOR THE SPIRITS THAT ROAM. THERE'S
DIPLOMACY, MIXED WITH A LITTLE BIT OF

FEAR. AS TWILIGHT DEEPENS, EVERYONE
COMES TO STANDSTILL, THEY DARE NOT AWAKEN
THE OTHERWORLDLY CREATURES THAT STALK THERE.
THERE ARE RULES, AND ONE DOES NOT WANT TO
STOMP AROUND IN UNCERTAIN LIGHT.BEST TO
BE QUITE AND HOLD YOUR BREATH AND CALL
ON THE ANCESTORS FOR PROTECTION.
BEST TO STAY HUMBLE AND SMALL AMONG

THE SHAPESHIFTERS. I THINK OF THEM OFTEN,
LAID OUT IN THE FAR MOUNTAINS OR IN CAVERNS.
THE HEARTH IN THE COURTYARD SIGNALING HOME.
I THINK ABOUT THEIR STORIES AND THE BELIEF
THEY HAD IN THE CREATOR. AND THE SPIRITUAL
THINGS, HOW ESSENTIAL THEY WERE TO
INSPIRATIONS OF PERSONAL POWER, LIKE THE
USE OF PEYOTE ON RESTRICTED LAND.

COUNTRY MAIDEN

AMISH COUNTRY PENNSYLVANIA. QUILTS
SOLD DOWN THE ROAD BY WOODEN RED
FARMHOUSES WHERE CHICKENS ROAM
FREE AND HORSE DRAWN CARRIAGES ARE THE
PREFERRED METHOD OF TRANSPORTATION.
THAT'S WHERE I SAW HERE, THE LITTLE
AMISH GIRL WITH PLATINUM BRAIDS AND
BIG BLUE EYES, EATING RASPBERRY BLUE


HARD CANDY BY THE POND, SURROUND BY
KITTENS AND DUCKS ALIKE. SHE ASKED ME
IF I WANTED ONE OF HER KITTENS. SHE SAID,
"THEY USUALLY WONDER OFF BY THE OPEN
ROAD AND GET RUN OVER BY THE CARS THAT
PASS BY HERE." I LOOKED AT THEM AND
HER, UNITED IN INNOCENCE, AND I THOUGHT
ABOUT HOW SHE ACCEPTED DEATH AS PART

OF LIFE. SHE WASN'T UPSET WHEN SHE TOLD ME
THAT. SHE HAD RECONCILED WITH IT, AND HER
DEMEANOR WAS CALM, MATTER OF FACT,
LIKE A MATURE COUNTRY MAIDEN. IN A
NEARBY SPOT ON THE FARM, FOUR OR FIVE
BOYS WERE PLAYING BY A DISCARDED
WAGON BEFORE BEING CALLED BACK TO CHORES.
THE LITTLE GIRL SENSED MY DISTRESS AT THE
QUESTION, AND SHE LOOKED AT ME AND SAID,

"YOU CAN HAVE AS MANY AS YOU WANT, THERE
ARE ALWAYS MORE BORN ON THIS FARM. AND I
CAN'T NAME THEM ALL." SHE SAT PERFECTLY,
WITH FOLDED ARMS UPON HER DRESS, LOOKING
UP AT ME. AND I THOUGHT ABOUT THE PROVERB
THAT SAYS, "A RIGHTEOUS MAN CARES FOR THE
NEEDS OF HIS ANIMALS." I SMILED AT HER AND
REPLIED, "I'LL TAKE TWO."

## HAPPY HIGHWAYS

I'VE TRAVELED TO MEXICO AND BEEN
DOWN HAPPY HIGHWAYS, HEADLIGHTS
BLARING IN THE GRINNING NIGHT. I'VE
HAD TEQUILA AND WHISPERED TO MEN
ABOUT FREE SPIRITS THAT ENJOY SOLITUDE.
AND I'VE BEEN INSINCERE AND SINCERE
ABOUT BEING INSINCERE.
THE COLORED LIGHTS THAT  ILLUMINATE

THE STREET VENDORS SELLING POTTERY
AND HANDWOVEN BASKETS, AND SILVER,
CALL TO ME. THEIR PIECES ARE HEALING
ART TO MY SOUL. I STILL LOVE THAT OFF
THE SHOULDER DRESS WITH EMBROIDERED
FLOWERS THAT MADE ME LOOK LIKE I
WAS FIFTEEN AGAIN, AND MY STATUE OF
OUR LADY OF GUADALUPE IS ONE OF A KIND.

I FEEL AT HOME IN MEXICO, IN THE BASILICA
THAT'S SINKING INTO THE GROUND AND HAS
BEEN FOR CENTURIES DUE TO ITS SOFT, CLAY-LIKE
SOIL. IT'S TOO UNSAFE TO GO THERE NOW,
BUT I STILL THINK ABOUT IT AND VISIT IT MY MIND,
AND WONDER ABOUT JUAN DIEGO WHEN HE FIRST
LOOKED INTO HER EYES. AND HOW WATERS CAN
DROWN YOU BEFORE LIFTING YOU UP ONCE AGAIN.

## WHAT FATED HER TO CHOOSE HIM

SHE LOVED HIM IN HER YOUTH
AND CARVED HIS NAME IN TREES,
WITH IDLE HOPES THAT STILL FLY
AND EASE HER PAIN. SHE WALKED
WITH HIM IN SALT WATER AS THE
WAVES KNOCKED THEM OFF THEIR
FEET,  IMMORTALIZING THE DAY
BEFORE NIGHTFALL.

SHE KISSED HIS LIPS WITH ONE
LAST GASP AND PAUSED AT HOW
PASSION LEFT THEM BOTH
SPEECHLESS. SHE KNELT BY HIS
SIDE AND STARED INTO HIS EYES,
INNOCENT AS SHE WATCHED HIM
SLEEP. IF LOVE IS AN ILL—ADVENTURE
THEN WHO IS TO BLAME FOR THAT?

THE NIGHT OF THE FIRE SHE RACED
TO THE SCENE, HE IN UNIFORM
DIDN'T EVEN KNOW SHE WAS THERE.
SHE CRIED HYSTERICALLY WHEN HE
ENTERED THE BURNING BUILDING
AND WHEN SHE DIDN'T SEE HIM COME
BACK OUT. I WATCH HER MOURN DAY AFTER
DAY AND ASK MYSELF,

"WHAT FATED HER TO CHOOSE HIM?"

# THE POWER OF SOUND

I'M THE PERFECT WITNESS TO
THE POWER OF SOUND, AND
HOW IT ECHOES AND RETURNS
REMORSELESS EVEN IN SLEEP.
I CAN HEAR A FLOCK OF BIRDS
UNIVERSAL IN THEIR NATURE
AND LAMENT, FLAP WITH THE
WIND AGAINST THE SKY.

I CAN HEAR MARTYRED BLOOD
SPEAK FROM THE HEAVENS.
AND HOW CLOCKS TICK, AND
TELL TIME. I CAN CRY IN THE
BROODING DARKNESS AND
SING AT THE MOON'S DEPARTURE.
I'VE SEEN HOW ROSES EMBRACE
LIBERTY,

AND HOW THEY CRUSH GRAPES
INTO WINE. I HEARD THE
SQUISHY SOUNDS THEY MAKE,
A LUSCIOUS AND DELICIOUS
THRILL. SAXOPHONES PLAY
IN AN ARTIST'S HANDS, AND ITS
NOISE IS LIKE A VULGAR TONE,
LIKE THE POWER OF SOUND

CALLED UP FROM A STORM.
THERE ARE MONSTROUS PITS
WHERE CREATURES YELL. AND
FLESHLY PLEASURES THAT MOAN
FROM THE UNKNOWN. AND
CHILDREN'S LAUGHTER COMING
FROM  CLOSED DOORS. MY EARS
ARE DESPERATE FOR ANYTHING,

ANY SOUND BUT SILENCE.

# TRADITION

TRADITIONAL CATHOLICS BELIEVE IN EVERYTHING
THAT EXISTED BEFORE THE SECOND VATICAN
COUNCIL. THE TRIDENTINE MASS, THE ROMAN
RITE LITURGY, THE CONSERVATIVE VIEW. THERE'S
NOTHING IN THIS WORLD THAT ISN'T CONFLICTED
IN ONE WAY OR ANOTHER. NOT EVEN GOD'S
HOLY CHURCH RUNS SMOOTHLY. I WONDER IF WE
SHOULD RENDER ALL NAMELESS, BECAUSE NAMING

AND LABELING ALWAYS BRINGS OUT TROUBLED
CHAOS. WE SHOULD ALL TAKE TENTATIVE STEPS
TOWARDS THIS, TOWARDS BEING VISIBLE YET
INVISIBLE. MAKE IT A CHOICE OF SOME KIND.
MY MIND SWARMS WITH EPHEMERAL SYLLABLES,
PRONOUNS BUZZING AND STINGING, HUMMING
AND CRAWLING, TUNNELING AWAY IN MY BRAIN.
I CAN ACCEPT ALL NAMELESS THINGS,

AND I DON'T MIND BEING NAMELESS MYSELF. I
DON'T NEED MY IDENTITY DEFINED. AND NEITHER
DOES GOD OR HIS CHURCH. YOU SEE, EVERYTHING
FITS. WE ARE AN INDIVIDUAL HUMANITY AS MUCH
AS A COLLECTIVE HUMANITY. AND THERE ARE MANY
TRADITIONS WE CAN HOLD DEAR. DO YOU EVER
WONDER WHAT THE COLOR OF EVERYTHING IS?  I KNOW
IT'S A RAINBOW OF INTENSITY AND CONVICTION.

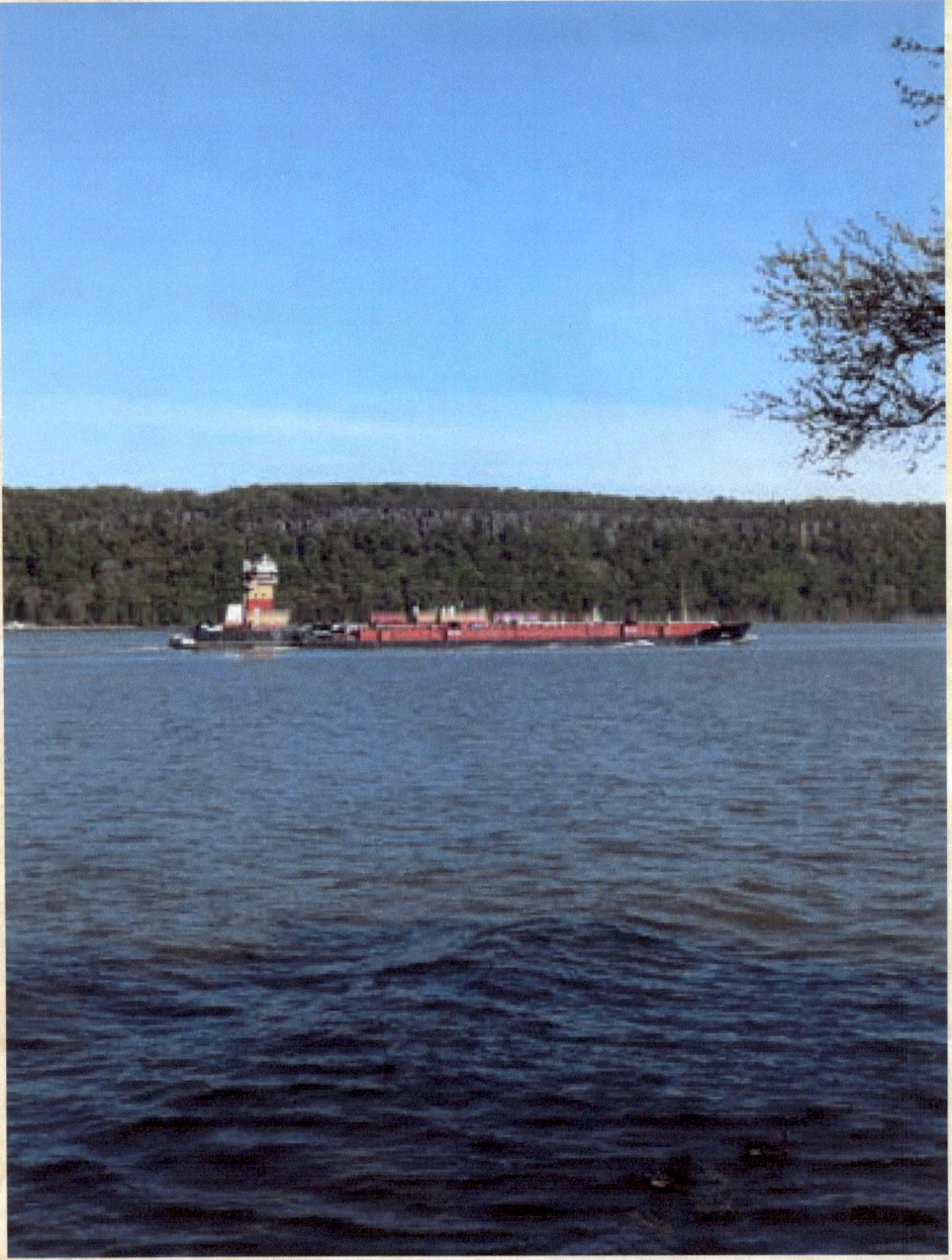

## GOD FINDS YOU

DEATH CLOSES IN ON US ALL,
AND IN OUR PATHS, IN OUR
QUESTS AND WORKS OF NOBLE
NOTES, THOSE DONE AND YET TO
BE DONE, WE PAY AN INNATE
HOMAGE TO THE LIGHTS THAT
BEGIN TO TWINKLE FROM WET
ROCKS, TO THE LONG DAYS AND
SLOW MOTION CLIMBS OF THE
MOON, TO THE TRAVELS AND THE
VESSELS THAT CARRY US. TO SAIL
BEYOND THE SUNSET IS EVERYONE'S
DREAM.  TO SEE WHAT THE OTHER
SIDE BRINGS IS OUR GRAB BAG OF
MYSTERY. WE ARE TAKEN, CLAIMED,
SPOKEN FOR; ALL OF US. WE CAN
LOOK FOR GOD AS THE TIDES LURE
US TO SLEEP WITH DRUNKEN
DELIGHT, OR WE CAN NEVER SEARCH
FOR HIM AT ALL. WE DON'T HAVE
TO BELIEVE IN ORDER TO BREATHE
OR TAKE IN LIFE. OUT THERE, AMONG
THE RISING AND SINKING STARS,
GOD FINDS US, AND CARRIES US HOME.

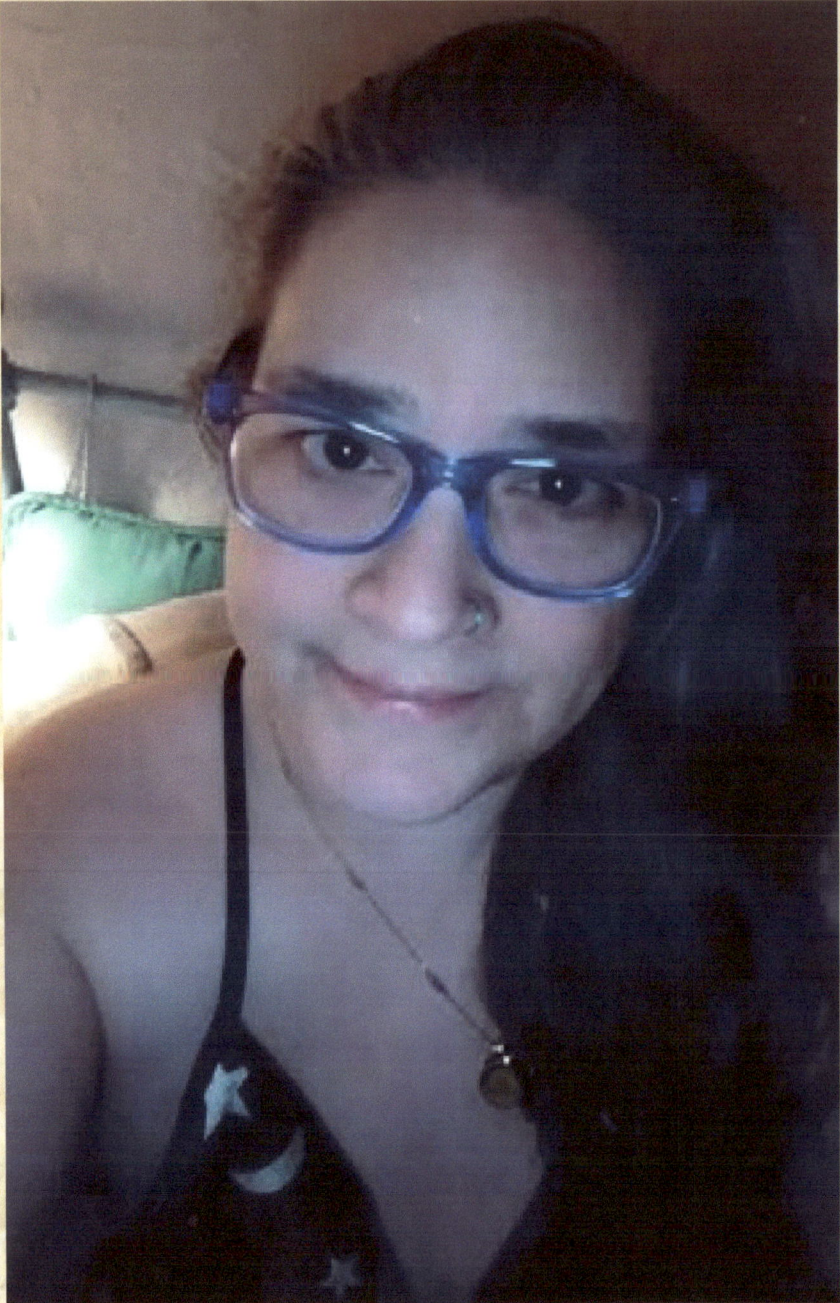

TERESITA IS MY BIRTH NAME. I BELIEVE THERE ARE MANY ROADS THAT LEAD TO GOD AND THAT GOD WILL EVENTUALLY FIND ME AND BRING ME HOME. AMEN!

I'D LIKE TO THANK MY PUBLISHER DUSTIN PICKERING OF TRANSCENDENT ZERO PRESS FOR HIS FRIENDSHIP, AND FOR BEING ONE OF THE BEST PUBLISHERS I HAVE EVER HAD.

I'D LIKE TO THANK BEN EADS FOR THE BLURB HE DID FOR ME AND FOR BEING SO KIND AND GENEROUS WITH HIS TIME. PLEASE CHECK OUT BEN'S BOOKS STARTING WITH CRACKED SKY AND HOLLOW HEART.

I'D LIKE TO THANK STEVEN L. SHREWSBURY FOR HIS BLURB AND FOR TAKING THE TIME TO READ MY WORK. YOU ARE AN AMAZING FRIEND! PLEASE CHECK OUT STEVEN'S BOOKS — RECKONING DAY, BLADESPELL, RED WAVES OF SLAUGHTER.

I'D ALSO LIKE TO THANK MICHAEL PENDRAGON — EDITOR AND PUBLISHER OF THE RENOWNED LITERARY HORROR JOURNAL, PENNY DREADFUL. YOU ARE SIMPLY THE BEST!

AND LAST BUT NOT LEAST I WOULD LIKE TO THANK SEAN DAVID HARVEY — AUTHOR AND GHOSTWRITER—SENIOR WRITER FOR A $40 BILLION BARRON'S TOP 10 FINANCIAL ADVISORY FIRM, FOR HIS REVIEW. YOU ARE AMAZINGLY KIND AND A BEAUTIFUL SOUL.

THIS BOOK IS DEDICATED IN ITS ENTIRETY TO JESUS CHRIST MY LORD AND SAVIOR, MY GOD!

THERE'S SO MUCH MORE I NEED TO SAY TO YOU. SO MUCH MORE I NEED TO TELL YOU.

TO ALL MY READERS, FAMILY AND FRIENDS, MAY YOUR JOURNEY BE BLESSED!

THERESA CECILIA GAYNORD IS AN OCCULT EXPERT, INTERNATIONAL AUTHOR, FORMER TEACHER—WHO'S WHO AMONG AMERICA'S TEACHERS 1993 AWARD. HER BOOKS ARE AVAILABLE FOR PURCHASE ANYWHERE BOOKS ARE SOLD.